Praise for *Quantu...*

CU00970927

"*Quantum Angel Healing* demonstrates that thoughts and emotions are able to affect the subtle information circuitry and intelligence of the subatomic particles constituting our cellular biochemistry. It is an integrative healing method and helpful link between quantum physics and spirituality."

> —Aeoliah, International Recording Artist/ Composer, Bestselling New Age Author, and Visual Artist

"Quantum Angel Healing is a new, effective method that shows us all how to use spiritual energy to reverse disease in our body, create lasting, nurturing relationships, and bring healing to our challenging world."

> —Brita Rupio, Artist, Author, and Quantum Angel Practitioner

"Quantum Angel Healing is a science-based healing method that uses spiritual energy to reduce pain and emotional blockages and to change limiting belief systems. A breakthrough in energy healing!"

> —Pascale Caroline Walder, Founder of Body Design® and Quantum Angel Practitioner

"Quantum Angel Healing uses techniques rooted in the science of quantum physics, which proves that the thoughts and belief systems of the observer influence the outcome of a situation. A fascinating and helpful tool for the healing of this world."

—Anja Löser, Master of Arts, Ayurvedic Massage Therapist, and Quantum Angel Practitioner

Quantum Angel Healing

Energy Therapy and
Communication with Angels

Eva-Maria Mora

Synergy Books

Quantum Angel Healing: Energy Therapy and Communication with Angels
Published by Synergy Books
P.O. Box 30071
Austin, Texas 78755

For more information about our books, please write us, e-mail us at info@synergybooks.net, or visit our web site at www.synergybooks.net.

Printed and bound in USA. All rights reserved. No part of this book may be reproduced by any mechanical, photographic, or electronic process, or in the form of a phonographic recording; nor may it be stored in a retrieval system, transmitted, or otherwise be copied for public or private use—other than for "fair use" as brief quotations embodied in articles and reviews—without prior permission of the author.

Publisher's Cataloging-in-Publication available upon request.

LCCN: 2010928101

ISBN-13: 978-0-9845040-1-5
ISBN-10: 0-9845040-1-X

Copyright © 2011 by Eva-Maria Mora, Amora Creations LLC

Illustrations: Stefanie Leja, Mannheim & Meike Müller, Hamburg

Foreign Rights: Random House GmbH, Germany: www.randomhouse.de

The information contained in this book reflects only the personal experience and views of the author. The intent of the author is only to offer information to help the reader in his or her quest for emotional and spiritual well-being. Readers are responsible to care for medical conditions under the direction of a physician. This book is not a substitute for the services of health care professionals. Proper care from a medical doctor should not be avoided, delayed, or discarded when there is a reason to consult a medical doctor. This book is not designed to diagnose, treat, or prescribe any illness or disease. Neither the author nor publisher is responsible for any consequences incurred by readers of this book or a Quantum Angel practitioner employing the remedies, exercises, meditations, or treatments reported herein. Any application of the material set forth in the following pages is at the reader´s discretion and his or her sole responsibility.

10 9 8 7 6 5 4 3 2 1

TABLE OF CONTENTS

Introduction xiii

Part 1
Theory and Practice xxi

Chapter 1
Formulating a Clear Intention 1
    Questions to Ask the Client 4
    Checking the Client's Beliefs 8
    Positive Beliefs for Therapists and Clients. . 10

Chapter 2
Communicating with the Angels 13
    Self-Confidence and Trust in God 16
    Accepting and Positive Belief Systems 17
    Love, Gratitude, and Kindness 17
    Forgiving Yourself and Others 20
    Prayers 22
    Crystals 23

Chapter 3
Cleansing the Energy Body 25
    Clinging, Disoriented Souls and Beings . . . 28
    Prepare for Meditation 31
    Meditation to Remove Disoriented
        Souls and Entities 32
    Protective Energy Techniques 34
    Etheric Cords 35

Cutting the Cords and Protection
   from Archangel Michael 39
Taking Salt Baths to Cleanse Your Aura. . . .41
Energy Techniques to Cleanse Your
   Home and Work Environment 43
Releasing Old Energies. 47

Chapter 4
Healing in Communication with the Angels **53**
Angel Breath 56
Treating Physical Pain. 60
Treating Emotional Pain and Blockages . . .61
Letting Go of/Replacing Fears
   and Limiting Belief Systems. 63

Chapter 5
The Chakra System and the Angels. **67**
The Color Spectrum of the Chakra System .69
The First Chakra .74
The Second Chakra. 74
The Third Chakra 75
The Fourth Chakra 76
The Fifth Chakra. 77
The Sixth Chakra 78
The Seventh Chakra 79
Chakra Clearing with the Archangels 79
Opening Your Energy Channels
   with Archangel Gabriel 82

Chapter 6
The Third Eye and the Pineal Gland **85**
Opening the Third Eye with Angel
Aura Crystals 88

Chapter 7

The Tasks of the Angels **93**

    The Archangels 96

    Cherubims and Seraphims 108

Chapter 8

Quantum Angel Reading **111**

    Preparation 113

    The Reading 116

    Asking the Angels about Yourself. 121

    Receiving Messages from the Angels 123

    Is It Genuine or Just My Imagination? 129

    Healing with the Angels 132

    Healing Cancer with the Power of

       the Angels 134

Chapter 9

The Power of Subconscious Programs **137**

    Self-Knowledge Is the First Step Toward

    Recovery. 139

    Is There Really a Difference Between

    Feelings and Emotions? 141

    Where Do Emotions Come From? 142

    Where Are Emotions Stored? 144

    What Is the Brain's Filter System? 146

    How Do Emotions Influence Our Lives? . .150

    How Can We Change Our Thoughts

    and Emotions? 153

    Checklist of Unwanted and

    Unresolved Emotions 154

Chapter 10
The Victim Program **161**
    Healing and Deleting the Victim
    Program with Archangel Chamuel. 167

Chapter 11
The Judge Program. **171**
    Healing and Deleting the Judge
    Program with Archangel Jophiel 174

Chapter 12
The "Unable to Forgive" Program **177**
    Healing and Deleting the "Unable
    to Forgive" Program with Archangels
    Jeremiel and Zadkiel. 178

Chapter 13
The "Love Hurts" Program **185**
    Healing and Deleting the "Love
    Hurts" Program with Archangel Raphael .186

Chapter 14
The Quantum Angel Healing Formula **191**
    Using the Quantum Angel
       Healing Formula 194
    Self-Rejection. 197
    Resistance. 198
    Lack of Self-Confidence 199
    Fear of Failure 199
    What Is Blocking My Success?. 200
    The Principle of Equalizing Energy Flows . 203
    How Does the Quantum Angel
       Healing Formula Work?. 205

Part 2
Illnesses and Symptoms **207**
       Code of Ethics for Quantum Angel
            Healing Practitioners 277

Bibliography **279**

About the Author **283**

ACKNOWLEDGMENTS

For
my son,
whose unconditional
love and wonderful light
supported me even in difficult times;
without him, this book would have never been written.

I thank all human and divine helpers, who
supported my work with love and patience. I thank
all my students and future readers of this book, who
are bringing more healing into this world.

My special thanks go to:
Dolores Saternus-Stenner
Michael Mora
Gerd Geselle
Cora Hughes
Gisela Arenas

INTRODUCTION

The most important question that humans ask is about their origin. In the course of evolution, humans got lost in the maze of their self-created illusions. Life is a maze with mirrors that reflect parts of us but do not permit us to see who we really are.

We search for solutions to our problems and for healing of our illnesses, focusing on others around us who might have the answers. We also blame others and find excuses for our miseries. "If I only had a better childhood...," we cry, or "If only my spouse had treated me better..." We identify with the roles that we play, and wear the corresponding masks. We identify with being homeowners, teachers, therapists, housewives, artists, employees, unemployed persons, retirees, club members, church members, patients, husbands, wives, mothers, and fathers. But is this really who we are?

No, these are only roles that we play. And behind the masks that we wear, we are hiding our fears and our pain. However, over the years, this only leads to disappointment and even more pain, which finally evolves into illnesses and difficult life situations.

Behind the mask and behind the pain that expresses itself at the physical, as well as at the emotional, level lurk the root and the cause of pain. It is on a deeper level than our hurt feelings and emotions or our traumatic experiences and illnesses; the origin of all pain is caused by our belief that we are separated from each other, from our true selves, and from God. This belief system generates deep fear: the energy from which all negative emotions are descended. Each of us has the task to restore the connection with our own God power and to remember who he or she really is.

As Gregg Braden scientifically proves in his book *The God Code*, we all have a "divine code" programmed into our DNA, into our genes; therefore we can find it in every cell of our bodies. Every person carries the power of God in every single cell of their body. And what kind of power is that? It is the power of love. Love generates the highest curative oscillation frequency in the universe—a divine frequency with which all problems can be solved and all illnesses cured.

It is normal that you might feel resistance against some of the things I share with you throughout this book. Just like in a yoga class, you start out with exercises that are very unusual for you, and you might stretch out more than you were expecting. Here you will find information, insights, and exercises that might be new and unusual for you as well. The first exercise, which I learned from my spiritual teacher, Zohar, was to stand in front of the mirror, look into my own eyes, and say to myself, *"I am the power of God for me."*

If you can say that without feeling uncomfortable in any way and just naturally feel the love of God within yourself, you have found a magic formula with which you can cure all illnesses and master all crises. You can say, for example, "I am the power of God for me, and I am healthy," or "I am the power of God for me, and I am happy and free." If you are able to stay—at any time and in every situation, 24-7—in pure God consciousness, which is the energy of unconditional love for yourself and all that is, you will need nothing else. You then will be enlightened like Christ, Buddha, or other spiritual masters. If you—like many of us—tend to forget who you really are and find yourself having problems or illnesses, the method that is explained in this book will help you a lot. With this method, you also will find access to your inner healer who has the creative power of the universe at his or her disposal. This inner healer can communicate with angels and be of great service to you and others.

Especially in difficult and changing times when so many things can be challenging, it is important to be able to help yourself, your family, and your friends. Since the earth is coming to the end of a cosmic cycle in the year 2012, which only happens every twenty-six thousand years, many people are questioning if this means we are facing an age of awakening or the end of the world as we know it. The Bible speaks about the time of Revelation. The Mayan calendar predicts 2012 as the end of an era on Earth. Other indigenous cultures, like the Hopis or Maoris, predict as well that 2012 will mark a critical shift in the history of our planet. No one knows exactly what is in store for us in 2012, but being prepared for any kind of difficult life situations or illnesses is more important now than ever before.

The good news is that every person is able to use and strengthen the natural healing energy in his or her hands and therefore is able to heal himself or herself and support others' self-healing as well. It is also comforting to know that every person is able to communicate with angels. These are by no means rare gifts but rather natural abilities, innate ones, even if they are mostly slumbering talents, which we only need to wake up and to tap into.

The universal life force energy has different names according to a certain culture. The Chinese call it "chi," the Japanese "ki," the Indians "prana," and the Germans speak of the "odem of the life." With the help of certain breathing and meditation techniques, it is possible for people to generate a high energy field and connect to an even higher energy field. The higher the frequency of the person concerned, the easier it will be to establish a discernible connection with angels. In this book, I will also speak about the angels' energy, which flows through the Quantum Angel Healing practitioner as a channel and is transmitted over his hands to the client.

In the book *Quantum-Touch: The Power to Heal,* the author, Richard Gordon, explains the fundamentals of energy healing (16ff.). I have studied with Richard for several years and also became one of the first Quantum Touch (QT) instructors in the United States. After I introduced the work to Europe and had been teaching many basic workshops as a QT teacher, more and more of my students told me that they had seen angels in my classes, who would support the basic energy work that my students were practicing. With respect to the QT curriculum, it was not possible to step outside and speak about angels and other realms at the time, although I was able to see angels and hear their messages.

However, the fundamentals of energy healing are valid for all different healing methods, no matter what they are called. This is simply because the universal law of resonance causes energy fields to adapt to each other. This happens at the subatomic or quantum-physical level. All people and particles in the universe are reacting accordingly. Richard explains in his book, that the law of resonance can be observed clearly if you put several big pendulum-type grandfather clocks on the same wall side by side, swinging out of phase to one another. Within only a few days, all pendulums will steadily swing in the same direction and beat together. In this example, the energy transference happens through the common wall (16). In other words, if two systems oscillate on different frequencies, the power of resonance will transfer energy from one to another. Through entrainment, which is a phenomenon that allows two similarly tuned systems to align their movement and energy, the two systems will match in rhythm and phase, so they will line up and vibrate at the same frequency. This also works with biological systems that might be out of tune and can therefore be used for healing treatments. It is important to notice that there are three different possible outcomes when two things or people are vibrating at different frequencies. Through resonance and entrainment, either the lower vibration will come up, the higher vibration will come down, or they will meet in the middle.

The purpose of the energy healing during a Quantum Angel (QA) treatment is to raise the vibration of the client who is in pain to the level of high energy, which is provided through the hands of the practitioner. The source of this high energy is not the practitioner's own life force energy, because this would unfortunately cause the practitioner to become energetically drained and eventually ill. The source of energy for QA practitioners is the unlimited divine love energy which is transferred through the angels. The practitioner, as well as the client, will resonate with this high vibrating source of energy. Quantum Angel Healing is much more than the actual energy healing part of the work, although just through that, I have seen many miracles happen in front of my eyes.

But what if people are not healing? What if something seems to be blocking them? What are the true causes of an illness or a difficult life situation? These were the questions I asked God and my angels. The answers came. They were the missing puzzle pieces that were not in any other healing modality that I had studied and practiced before. The angels introduced me to a fascinating method, and with their profound wisdom, they showed me how specific meditations, visualizations, and the deletion of old programs and belief systems were able to transform harmful emotional energies, which led to lasting healing.

There was so much more to experience in the world of Quantum Angel Healing than I ever could imagine. The angels were experts in quantum physics and had answers for all questions, illnesses, difficulties, and challenges that my clients were facing. With their help, it became easy to understand the scientific part of the work and to identify and transform the true cause of a problem. It became clear to me that I had received a special gift, a new healing method with tools for a new paradigm, which I was meant to share with humanity.

The tools of previous eras of medicine (the first was drugs and surgery; the second was mind-body medicine) lacked integration into this deeper understanding of reality, where science and spirituality are two sides of the same coin. The angels explained to me that the Medicine of the Third Era incorporates fundamental concepts of what scientists call quantum physics:

1. The observer effect: The act of measuring or observing an object profoundly alters its state. In effect, the observer creates his or her own reality

2. Quantum entanglement: In quantum entities, a property of one particle (e.g., spin) automatically and instantaneously determines the corresponding property of the other particle—irrespective

of their distance from one another. Leading-edge scientists are convinced that these quantum-information channels are how our cells communicate with one another. These findings are already being applied in quantum computing.

3. Nonlocality: The nonlocal mind (consciousness) is able to transmit to and receive information from other people and is infinite in space-time.

Medicine of the Third Era applies these principles to perform healing at a distance, diagnostic intuition, clairvoyance, telepathy, energy healing, and prayer. It goes beyond physical death and integrates nonphysical helpers (e.g., angels) in the process. Quantum Angel Healing is a new method centered in this Third Era of Medicine. It provides tools for working with the unseen worlds and explains how to accelerate healing and transformation in all areas of life.

My mission to share Quantum Angel Healing became very clear when, to my great surprise, I was approached by Random House Europe to write a book about my work, which until that day had never crossed my mind. My book, *Quantum Angel Healing*, became a bestseller in Europe. I have taught thousands of people how to connect and communicate with their angels and how they can access the divine matrix—a cosmic database, a quantum field—where all answers to health issues and difficult situations can be found. There are no restrictions to time and space. The angels taught us that if we are experiencing an imbalance, we can connect with them through the "Angel Breath" and apply the "Angelic Healing Formula" to rearrange these quantum phenomena and regain health. It does take a higher divine source of energy to effectively transform any emotions, thoughts, patterns, and programs that underlie ill health. The divine source and God power can be found in each of us: the practitioner is a channel and conduit for healing energy, the patient is the actual healer, and the angels are our "heavenly doctors."

Random House Europe has published many of my books and transformation CDs over the last years. It is my heart's desire now to share this work in English with everybody in my beloved country of choice—the USA—and the rest of the world.

Part 1

Theory and Practice

The greatest illness of our time is to be unwanted, unloved, and left alone.
—*Mother Teresa (1910–1997), ambassador of love for the poor and sick, Nobel Peace Prize winner*

CHAPTER 1

Formulating a Clear Intention

It is more difficult to destroy a preconceived opinion than an atom.

—*Albert Einstein (1879–1955), German physicist and Nobel Peace Prize winner*

At the beginning of each healing session, it is important to set a clear intention. Ways to formulate an intention are explained on page 9. Before a Quantum Angel Healing (QAH) practitioner can help a client set an intention, it is necessary to ask a few background questions, based on the client's story. This will help the client to become more aware, so they can understand why a problem or an illness possibly occurred. This question might be unexpected, and may sometimes cause resistance from a new client, but it is a true eye-opener.

"How does this problem or this illness serve you?"

Some clients might block the answer to this question and spontaneously say, "It doesn't!" because they are not aware of their own creation. However, the bad news for

1

a client is that they created the situation themselves—even if they don't realize it. The good news is that during a QAH treatment, the true cause of the problem will become apparent.

I remember a session with a client from fifteen years ago. At that time, I did not ask the important question up front. Here is the story:

Anna, age sixty, had an appointment with me for an energy treatment. Her hands were hurting badly, which was causing her problems at work. Every day she sat at the computer and the movement of her typing fingers brought tears to her eyes. She was convinced that the pain was caused by arthritis.[1]

After I had worked with Anna for twenty minutes, the pain was gone and she seemed to be happy. Ten days later, she called again, complaining that the pain in her hands had come back. She booked another appointment. I was guided by the angels to ask Anna, "How does this situation or symptom serve you?"

Anna told me about her job in the big office of an insurance company, where she had been working for twenty-five years. Her job was to input the data of every customer who'd had a car accident. As an intuitive person, she felt the pain of the injured people. Anna was very unhappy at work and frustrated about sitting at the computer eight hours a day, five days a week. The added stress caused by her coworkers made the situation unbearable. Her heart's desire was to quit her job, but she believed she could not support herself any other way, and so she stayed

---

1. Please *do not* accept the diagnosis of your client. It might be their own opinion or imagination, or it might be the opinion of a well-meaning friend, neighbor, relative, or doctor. Listen to the guidance of the angels and your own intuition from your higher self.

at her job for financial reasons. Every day she said to herself, "Only five more years to retirement."

What can we learn from this example? Anna's desire to quit her job was contrary to her preconceived notion that she needed to work another five years at that job to afford retirement. This conflict was expressed through Anna's body, which reacted with pain. Pain is always an indicator that a person is out of balance and that the body, mind, and soul are struggling with each other.

The question "How does this symptom serve you?" could be answered easily with, "If my hands hurt, I cannot do this work—and I really do not want to work anymore."

In this case, the angels helped to identify Anna's limiting belief system—"I have to work at the insurance company to make a living"—and transferred the negative energy to her body. Realizing this had a powerful impact on Anna's life. Not only did her body heal itself and her pain disappear for good, but Anna was able to free her mind from the limiting belief system and became more open-minded. She listened to the angels' messages and their advice, which were communicated to me in telepathic words and pictures. During our treatment, I shared with Anna that the angels showed me a picture of silver coins and then they said, "father," which did not make any sense to me.[2] Anna looked at me with surprise, for she had forgotten all about the silver coin collection which she had inherited from her father. Twenty boxes of coins were stored in the basement of her house. She had never unpacked the boxes and had no clue what

---

2. During thousands of treatments I have learned to pass on the angelic messages just the way I receive them. I will explain in chapter 8 how this works.

the coins were worth. Anna saw an expert and got an appraisal for her coin collection, which turned out to be very valuable. She sold the collection at an international auction, and it was easy for her to financially bridge the five years to her retirement. She even felt energetic enough to work part-time, helping children with their homework. She loves working with children. She is now completely pain-free and happy.

Questions to Ask the Client

To get a feel for the hidden causes of a problem or an illness, the following questions are very helpful. These suggestions are not meant to be followed strictly, but are highly recommended.

1. When did this problem or illness start?
2. Have you ever experienced a similar situation before?
3. How does this problem affect your daily life at home? At work? At school?
4. What can you not do because of this issue?
5. How do your family members react to this situation? Do they help you?
6. In what way does this situation or illness serve you? What benefit do you gain from it? What consequence does it have?
7. What will you do when the situation has been resolved and the symptoms are gone?
8. How will your family members and friends react when you are suddenly healthy, happy, abundant, and free?

9. What does the desired result of this treatment look like to you? Describe it as a picture.

10. What will be your next step? How do you feel?

Another interesting story about self-serving ill-nesses happened in my own family. My husband and I attended a small family reunion in Germany. My aunt and other family members had not seen me since I'd left Germany and moved to the United States. My life change was very suspicious to them and while we were sitting at a table having coffee and cake, they asked as many questions as they could. *What exactly are you doing now? What is energy healing with angels? It sounds pretty much like hocus pocus. Is that why you got your two master's degrees at the university?*

No matter what my husband and I explained about energy work and healing, they still shook their heads at me. I could clearly feel their rejection, criticism, and dis-appointment in my life's choices. After the conversation ended, the male family members left the table and went to investigate the backyard. My aunt got stuck with the dirty dishes, and I decided to help her clean the table. All of a sudden, she looked around to make sure nobody could see us and then she said, "Psst. Come here. Do whatever it is you do to my foot!" She put her leg up on the couch and showed her toe to me, which was bent, deformed, and painful. It grew over the toe next to it and my aunt could not wear normal shoes.

Of course, I was willing to do a treatment on her. At that time, however, I was still inexperienced and not really prepared to do a session on the spot. I did not ask her how her toe situation served her. Instead, I started with the energy treatment immediately. My aunt continued to make sure that nobody saw us, as if we were doing something weird, forbidden, sinful, or criminal. After a few minutes, my aunt yelled at me, "Ouch! What is going on?" The toe reacted to the healing energy and moved back into its normal, natural position. This movement simply caused temporary discomfort, which is normal for deformed bones during the process of alignment.

At this very moment, my husband entered the room. He was looking for me and witnessed the alignment of my aunt's special toe. He and I were really happy about the healing, as it would spare my aunt from having an operation that was scheduled for the following week.

Now, do you think this is a story with a happy end? Not really! As soon as my aunt comprehended that the toe was perfectly fine and an operation would not be necessary, she said, "That can't be! That's impossible. I can't believe this."

My aunt's disbelief had the same impact as a negative affirmation, especially with the intense emotional energy with which she expressed it. The toe reacted promptly and bent back over the toe next to it. This is how my aunt created the same "unpleasant situation" again.

You might now ask yourself, why did this happen? Let's take a closer look at my aunt's story and her family situation. My aunt endured several difficulties in her life, including having both of her hips replaced. Her hip surgery was painful, but it also had its benefits: a new cleaning lady was hired, her husband was very attentive and brought her flowers on a regular basis, and friends and relatives called every day to ask, "How are you? Is there anything I can do for you?" With her upcoming toe operation, she actually had the chance to get that much attention again, for an even lesser price. It was just the toe pain she had to sacrifice this time.

Paying for love with pain is a very common subconscious activity that I will talk about more later in this book (the love hurts program). My aunt did not want to miss out on the "good deal" she was going to get again the week after our visit because of my hocus pocus energy work. It took me a while to realize that she did not really want her symptom to go away, but she simply wanted attention—including mine. She felt that if she could share her misery with someone, she could benefit and at least get a hug.

So again, please don't forget to ask the important question, for it might be that a client may not be interested in getting well. From the client's perspective, it might be that they think they would eventually miss out on secondary benefits, like attention (which is also mistaken as a form of love), if they were to heal. Unfortunately, the patient-therapist paradigm of the past was often based exactly on fulfilling therapists' and doctors' financial needs first, and patients' needs second. Just think about that for a moment.

A patient doesn't always want to get well. The fear of change plays a key role in many situations. To avoid frustration when treating a client, it is important to first clarify what the benefit of healing will be and what a person will have to give up (e.g., an interesting story, special treatment, or a mysterious illness). There are many reasons why people don't heal that are independent of the healing method or medication they try.

Not until there is a clear picture of the result a treatment will have, including positive emotions like happiness, joy, ease, and love, will complete and spontaneous healing be possible and successful. Subconscious programming, belief systems, and suppressed emotions can prevent a person from getting better or healing completely. As soon as certain unconscious belief systems and their corresponding energies dominate a human being—no matter how good the intentions of a therapist are—not much will be achieved. It is like driving a car with one foot on the gas and one foot on the brake.

Checking the Client's Beliefs

Listen carefully to your client's story and check to see if they have the following belief systems or fears:

1. I deserve to be ill.
2. I am unable to reach my goal and I can't change it anyway. I don't have the strength or power to do this.
3. Change is a threat. It scares me.
4. God punishes me with this illness. He does not want me to get well.
5. Life is a struggle.
6. I inherited this illness. It is in my family's genes. It was unavoidable that I would get it too.
7. Suffering, pain, and financial difficulties are part of spiritual growth.
8. Regular doctor's visits, operations, and medications are a part of my life.
9. I have tried everything. No one can really help me.
10. Angels and divine powers don't exist.

When your client is ready to look at their hidden, limiting belief systems, start working with the Angelic

Healing Formula found in chapter 14. As a QAH practitioner, you will help your client set a clear intention. It is very important to pay attention to little negating words like "no" or "not." The subconscious mind does not hear these words. When a client sets the intention, "I do *not* want to smoke anymore," the subconscious hears, "I want to smoke more." It is better to say instead, "My life is free of cigarettes." When a client says, "I do not want to have pain anymore," his subconscious mind hears, "I want to have more pain." Better wording would be, "I feel good, and I am healthy." Negative affirmations actually strengthen the energy of that which you want to let go.

Pay attention to how many times during the day you use the word "not" and talk about what should stop in your life and what you don't want. Be mindful and express what you want. This is especially important for parents, who want to tell their children what they want them to do. Formulating your sentences in a positive way and telling your children what they should be doing, rather than what they shouldn't, will have much better results. Instead of saying, "Don't scream so loudly," say, for example, "Speak quietly."

Before every QAH treatment, it is not only necessary to check the belief systems of a client, but also of the practitioner. How would you feel, and what would you think, if a cancer patient had the clear intention to transform and dissolve his tumor with the help of the angels? Let's say he is ready for complete healing. Are you? Do you believe that this is possible? What would you do as a client if you could sense the doubts and fears of a therapist? My recommendation is that you find a person with substantial experience in this field of healing work and whose belief system has a positive impact on your intention to get well.

It is important that a practitioner has a positive expectation on the outcome of a session, an open mind, and an open heart, as well as the willingness to surrender and allow anything to happen. The ideal practitioner understands that every human being has divine power and the potential to use their own abilities for self healing, and will include God's and the angels' help. If a practitioner does not have experience with a certain problem, situation, or illness, it is of even more importance that they are open and know that miracles are possible.

Positive Beliefs for Therapists and Clients

1. I do not know if it is possible to heal this, but I am open for it to happen.

2. Every human being has a powerful soul. It is the power of God.

3. The information for perfect health is stored in every cell of the body. It can be activated at any time.

4. The body has its own healing powers and wisdom.

5. I am free of all blocking energies, thoughts, and emotions.

6. God and the angels work through me.

7. I can feel and sense energy.

8. I can communicate with the angels.

9. I trust the process and accept improvement and healing.

10. There is always a solution. Spontaneous healing is possible.

If the intention for the QAH treatment is set clearly, and disturbing energies of any form, including negative and limiting belief systems, are transformed, the practitioner, the client, and the angels pull in one direction. Unwanted energies and their symptoms have no chance to stay.

CHAPTER 2

Communicating with the Angels

Angels are messengers from God. They come in many forms, colors, and sizes. They are mostly invisible to the human eye. We can compare them with invisible TV or radio waves, which are always there. We know that we can only receive TV and radio signals as pictures or sounds once we turn on a receiver and choose a station which is broadcast on a certain frequency. All humans have an internal "Angel Receiver," which they can turn on to hear, feel, smell, see, or become aware of the angels around them.

It is very important to quiet the mind before communicating with the angels; this can be done with meditation or simply in a moment of silence. The Angel Receiver gets stronger if you purify your body of toxins, get enough sleep, and exercise on a regular basis. It helps to have an open mind, to stop doubting and judging, and to know that angels are all around you.

You can invite the angels to contact you, and you can ask for a repeated sign that you recognize. For example, you can ask them to leave you a feather or coin, or show you a license plate on a car with "444," which is the angels' number. The angels are very cooperative, and they are committed to help and support you at any given time. Simply ask them to help you with anything, including the so-called little things in life.

Don't be afraid to call upon them. God created millions of angels. They can be in many places, any time, simultaneously. However, they love and respect you too much to interfere with your free will. If you're specific and ask for what you really want, it will happen.

The clearer our energy field and the higher our oscillation frequency, the easier we can receive the messages of the angels.

The most effective methods to raise our own frequency are introduced in detail on pages 16 ff.; however, let's start with a few more words about communicating with the angels.

Communication with the angels, the ambassadors of God, can occur in many different ways. A lot of people receive divine messages nonverbally, by internal pictures, voices, or feelings. They simply know some things without being able to explain them. Others dream about foreboding events or receive messages in their dreams. The angels give us signs, and we can ask for additional signs if needed.

My angels often leave me pennies as a token of their presence. I have found these coins at the most impossible places and in the most interesting situations. I remember that I found two shiny pennies on the tiny inside frame of the drop-off box for rented movies. My husband and I returned the DVDs before we drove from Phoenix to Los Angeles. I knew the angels had placed the pennies there to take with us. I strongly felt their presence during this road trip and knew we were protected, guided, and safe. If I am just on my way to an important appointment or think about something special and need an answer, a penny will suddenly appear right in front of me. Some people find white feathers; others get messages from songs on the radio. Pay attention also to repeating numbers, for example, on the license plates of the cars in front of you; they often contain coded messages. The number 444 is meant to remind you that the angels travel with you.

For most people, it is difficult to have the awareness that they are always surrounded by angels. They would like to feel, see, and hear their messages, but do not really believe that this is possible. This belief has to do with the social programming that many people subconsciously received while growing up. For example, if the parents and teachers who educated a child do not believe that angels exist, a child will accept and share the same belief system. All incoming data (including angel messages) have to pass an "editor" in our brain. The editor is like a software program in a computer. (More about subconscious beliefs and programs in chapter 9.) A "human software program" that contains limiting belief systems from our social programming does not allow information about the angels to be passed on to our higher brain functions, which are connected to our awareness. If this happens, we will therefore simply not register the subtle messages that the angels send us.

However, with some practice, it is not only possible, but easy to receive messages from the angels, especially if you have an open mind and raise your own frequency.

The following will help you raise your own frequency:

Self-confidence and trust in God

Accepting and positive belief systems

Love, gratitude, and kindness

Forgiveness for both self and others

Prayers

Crystals

Energetic clearing

Angel Breath (see Chapter 4, pages 55 ff.) and energy healing

Self-confidence and Trust in God

Gaining self-confidence is a process that might take some time. Many people suffer from constant fears and believe that they are not good enough, or "perfect." Others, who have a huge ego, believe they are the greatest or that there is no one better than them. These beliefs are a coping mechanism to cover up fears and vulnerability. Some people switch between the two extremes; they are sometimes depressive and other times manic. People judge themselves and others according to the standards in their specific social environment.

"Know thyself" is one of the inscriptions on the walls of the Temple of Apollo in Delphi, Greece. The wisdom of this phrase is as important today as it was in ancient Greece. A healthy self-confidence means knowing your own strengths and weaknesses and understanding that we all are equal, unlimited, and valuable divine beings.

However, to trust in your own God-given powers and abilities requires you to transform the energy of negative emotions and to delete your identification with limiting belief systems and programs. It is important to heal old wounds, to let go of all illusions, and to understand who you really are.

Accepting and Positive Belief Systems

Accepting what is and knowing everything happens for a reason according to the divine plan, are the first steps to being open-minded. With an open mind and a positive attitude—no matter how difficult a situation might seem—everything is possible, including miracles and healings. Please recognize the many miracles of life everywhere around you. You can look at nature, a baby, or your own body and be grateful for everything.

The angels can help you in your daily life or during a healing session. Miracles will happen. Understand that you are not responsible for how, why, or when miracles or healings happen.

Love, Gratitude, and Kindness

Be kind and loving to yourself and others. The energies that you send out by being loving and kind will dissolve possible disharmony and conflict. Make an effort to consciously be friendly, loving, and kind to everyone you meet. People will be very grateful for your kindness—it is like the sun is shining in a cold and dark place. Your loving behavior changes the frequency around you. It is very important to stay in that frequency, because you will notice a difference in how great you feel at the end of the day.

Are you currently facing a difficult life situation in which it is almost impossible for you to feel love and gratitude? Then please remember other difficult situations in your life and how you mastered them. Think of all situations that have not turned out the way you would have liked: your first F in school, your first heartbreak, a canceled engagement, a serious illness, or a financial crisis through extended unemployment. And then remember how everything turned out for good: Since the first F, you have done the utmost to study properly and have only received good grades. The first heartbreak released unexpected creativity within you. If the engagement had not been canceled at that time, you would never have gotten to know your current partner—who matches you so much better. The serious illness changed your whole life positively, and you have overcome the financial crisis. After the interview and the rejection letter, you have received a better offer for a great career opportunity.

Make a list of all situations and events which were at first difficult and disappointing for you, but which turned out to be a blessing in the end. What miracles have you experienced in your life?

The reasons for illnesses and crises are often disclosed to us long after the situation is resolved. However, imagining that we are healthy and that all is well in the middle of a crisis will help us energetically manifest exactly that. While we do this intensely—feel our situation with deep gratitude and love—our energy changes and, with it, our reality.

Mary lives in the Arizona desert. Her house is far out and almost fifty miles away from the nearest city. She has solar electricity and her own well, which helps her to survive in the merciless heat of the desert. One year was especially hot; it did not rain for many months and her well dried out. Mary decided to meditate every day. She visualized clouds and rain, while feeling deep gratitude for the refreshing rain that she could feel on her skin during the meditation. Her friends thought she must be crazy when she told them about her daily practices. They were concerned about her and tried to talk her into moving to the city. Mary did not change her daily habit of meditating and actually feeling the outcome of what she was envisioning.

After ten days of meditating, clouds started to come in. The clouds became thicker and darker, the wind picked up, and finally thunder and lightning announced the arrival of a big storm with heavy rainfall. It rained the whole night and the groundwater filled her well. Mary's meditation was not simply wishful thinking, but co-creating with the universe, using the same techniques the Native Americans did for thousands of years.

Meditation has worked for my other clients as well. After the divorce from her husband, Lori kept the house, which was in pretty bad condition. She was in desperate need of money. Her mortgage payments were three months behind, and the house needed a new roof. Lori had no savings, and the bank started sending unfriendly letters. A good friend shared with Lori the important principle of love and gratefulness. It made sense to her, and she practiced every day. She felt deep gratitude and love while visualizing the moment of paying off her house loan in full. Every day, she trusted that her vision would become her reality, and she meditated without any doubt or fears. After seven days of meditating, her brother in Texas gave her a call. He had won the lottery and offered her $30,000—enough money to cover her mortgage.

Forgiving Yourself and Others

Your own feelings of guilt and your inability to forgive are heavy energies. They are weighing you down like lead around your ankles. Those energies are also lowering your frequency. If you clear your energetic field by freeing yourself from guilt and forgive yourself and others, you strengthen your immune system and your ability to be aware of subtle energies. Your clairvoyance and intuition also become much stronger.

The next exercise will help you clear unwanted blocking energies from your chakra system. By forgiving yourself and others, you can experience more inner peace, harmony, and balance. It is really important to transform and release the energies on all levels and not just say the words.

Inventory

With a pen and paper, make a list with the names of all the people (dead or alive) who have treated you badly or hurt your feelings. Write down the names of those people you believe you already have forgiven. Start with your family members. There are different levels of forgiveness, and sometimes the deeper emotional levels and their energetic impact have not been dealt with yet. Your list might also include pets; write down their names as well.

Releasing Energies and Forgiveness

Make sure that you are in a quiet space where no one will disturb you. Breathe deeply, in and out. Calm and relax yourself as if you were getting ready to meditate. Close your eyes and visualize an image of each person on your list that you can project onto a golden, light-filled screen. Go through each name on your list and envision their picture on the imaginary screen. Say to each person, "I forgive you with all my heart and release the binding energies between us on all levels. I ask the angels to transform the energies into love. I am free, and you are free." Then you proceed with the next picture.

The time it takes to forgive each person will vary—some will be long, some will be quick. Allow all of your emotions and feel them being released from your energy field. Take your time with this process. If you cannot finish your list in one session, continue another day. Some people do this exercise for weeks or months.

Karen had been suffering from severe migraine headaches since she was seven years old. She told me the long story of all the therapies she had gone through and that she could not function without taking strong pain medication. During our energy treatment, Karen was able to relax. The angels' healing energies helped to reduce the pain, and their messages were comforting to Karen. The angels mentioned her father, and when I passed the messages on to Karen, many inner pictures came up and she remembered difficult situations from her childhood. She cried a lot, and with the tears, tension was released from her body.

Karen and I talked about her unhappy childhood. Her father belonged to the German military and raised his daughter like a drill sergeant. Without being aware of it, Karen lived her life ruled by the "good-girl-program" Even as an adult, it was difficult for her to express her wants and needs—she had been suppressing them all her life. These suppressed, conflicting energies were the main cause of her headaches.

I asked her if she was ready to transform the negative energies that she had stored in her chakra system for over forty-five years. She said that she was ready for transformation and healing. We continued our healing session with the angels, who guided her through a healing meditation. After the treatment, Karen was a little tired, but her headache was gone. She called me after a month, feeling much better, energetic, and free of medications and headaches. It was a miracle to her, and she was very grateful.

Prayers

Many scientific studies and medical research have shown that the power of prayer has a positive impact on curing illnesses, solving conflicts, and even the growth of plants. Some of the most profound results that show the impact of prayer on plants have been achieved by the Findhorn Foundation in Scotland. A close friend of mine spent the whole summer in Findhorn, where she worked in the foundation's gardens. Her work included daily prayers and contact with the angels and nature spirits who were also "helpers" in the gardens. My friend told me about her many conversations with the flower angels (devas). She took pictures of the beautifully blooming flower gardens and the abundance of vegetables—which grew bigger in those gardens than anywhere else in Scotland.

For more than two decades, Spindrift Research in Oregon conducted laboratory experiments to illustrate the effects of prayer under scientific conditions. In countless successful experiments, the researchers investigated the growth of plants, yeast, mold, etc., in conjunction with prayer. The group's results offer compelling evidence for the positive effects of prayer, consciousness, and spiritual healing.[1]

In 1,500 experiments, Daniel Benor documented the positive, healing impact of prayer.[2] So did Larry Dossey

1. www.spindriftresearch.org
2. Daniel Benor, *Healing Research: Holistic Energy Medicine and Spirituality* (Munich: Helix, 1992).

in his book *Healing Words.* In his other book, *Be Careful What You Pray For...You Might Just Get It,* Dossey states that it is possible to create unwanted situations if the intentions of your prayers are not clear.[3] Therefore, it is very important to be specific and to avoid negative concepts in your prayers.

Many times, people ask me if there is a right or a wrong way to pray. My answer is, "Right is whatever feels right to you." There are many different prayers and different religions; I respect all of them. To me, prayer is the personal language of the heart talking to the highest source of love, which has many different names in different cultures around the world. My prayer consciousness has shifted; I no longer ask for something. It is the opposite. I express my heartfelt gratitude for the many blessings that I have already received. I don't take my health and my life for granted—which I still did when I was younger. However, I do ask for support with certain projects or potentially difficult situations and hand them over to God and the angels. I ask for my heart and mind to be open so I can give and receive divine love. I trust very much that by sending out love, answers will come and everything will turn out for the best and good of all.

Crystals

Quartz crystal is a powerful energy conductor mainly used in electronic equipment, medical apparatus, watches, TV sets, etc. The purpose of crystal is to receive and transmit signals. In radios, they are used to receive and stabilize a

---

3. Larry Dossey, *Be Careful What You Pray For...You Might Just Get It* (New York: HarperOne, 1998).

signal from a certain radio station on a very precise frequency. Quartz crystals are piezoelectric; they generate an electric field or potential, especially under pressure or in response to a change in temperature.

If a person is wearing or holding a crystal which is vibrating on the high frequency of the angels (angel aura crystal), it is much easier to intensify communication with the angels. The high energy field also supports the self-healing process. Over many centuries, alchemists used crystals for transformation and to attract positive energies.

Crystals also absorb subtle energies of all kinds, for example, the energy of negative thought forms. A quartz crystal is both an energy shield and an energy filter for the wearer. Like any other filter, crystals need to be cleared of the energies that they might have absorbed on a regular basis. To clear your crystal, simply set an intention for the crystal to be cleared in a little prayer and put the crystal in bright sunlight for three to four hours. You could also ask the angels to clear the crystal from any negative or harmful energies with their beautiful, divine light. On pages 96 ff., you can find more information about archangels and their corresponding crystals.

CHAPTER 3

Cleansing the Energy Body

Energy can never disappear.
—Hermann von Helmholtz, German physiologist and
physicist (1821–1894)

Every contact with energies, human or spirit, leaves an energetic imprint. Every emotional vibration, e.g., those expressed through human speech or thought, has a different imprint and impact on matter, including the human body. The human body mainly consists of water, which is relevant if we take a look at the interesting research of Dr. Masaru Emoto. Dr. Emoto directed energy to water through speech, thoughts, and written notes attached to a container of water. He took droplets from this water and froze the different samples. The resulting water crystals were either harmonious or had sharp edges, depending upon whether the words or thoughts were positive (e.g., peace, love, gratitude) or negative (e.g., war, hatred, chaos). Dr. Emoto claims that the different crystalline structures of frozen water can also be achieved through prayer or music.

All objects that you come in contact with—all buildings, houses, and rooms that you enter or live in—have an energetic imprint. Rooms in which you feel uncomfortable usually have an energetic residue that is not in harmony with your vibration. If this is the case, an energetic clearing would certainly help (see pages 43 ff.).

Hospitals, cemeteries, airports, trains, buses, churches, department stores, and other public places with high traffic have a multitude of different energetic imprints. They are also favored by earthbound spirits and other spirit beings who can attach themselves to humans. If the frequency of your energy body is low and/or your aura is weakened—which can be a result of stress—it is very likely that you can pick up "hitchhikers." At first, this goes unnoticed. A good comparison is the moment of infection with bacteria and viruses. The symptoms of the infection do not show immediately, but are very apparent a little while later.

A strong and clear energy body, which is also called an "aura," is like a natural protective shield or energetic immune system. In many cases, however, this shield has holes which enable earthbound spirits to enter the aura of a person and attach themselves. The consumption of alcohol and drugs attracts earthbound spirits who had a problem with these addictions when they were still alive. Like attracts like is very true in this case. Stress, fear, and negative emotions and thoughts, as well as insufficient energetic clearing, make a person very susceptible to energy vampires.

An energy attachment can also lead to physical symptoms like pain or illnesses. Very often, they exhibit first as emotional imbalances, e.g., sadness, depression, or anger, which occur for no obvious reason. The specifics of the unexplainable emotion depend on the emotional state of the soul or spirit attached to a human. You need to be aware of which emotion is your own, and which emotion is very strange for you (not to be mistaken with PMS, which is due to hormonal imbalances).

A human being can be a host or source of energy for an earthbound spirit. The life force energy of the host is used by the spirit—also known as an energy vampire. You probably also know living people who are energy vampires and who can really drain your energy when talking to you. If this is the case, I recommend an energetic cord cutting with Archangel Michael (pages 39 ff.). You will feel a difference in energy level.

We all wash our hands many times a day. We shower, bathe, and change our clothes on a regular basis, but we forget to clear our energy body and chakra system (pages 79 ff.). A dense and uncleared energy body is one of the main causes for emotional imbalances and illnesses. We can distinguish many forms of energetic attachments with negative impacts from the spirit world; not all spirits are beloved relatives from the other side or angels!

An intentional contact with the spirit world or ghosts by people who are untrained and inexperienced can cause a lot of harm and damage. Someone who plays with a Ouija board or tarot cards or participates in table tipping, just for fun, is in danger of becoming possessed by a spirit without being aware of it. Please be careful not to contact any unprofessional medium or psychic for a reading. They might have messages for you, but do not know "who is who" in the spirit world and can be in contact with harmful entities or demons. Possible signs for the presence of a negative entity, earthbound spirit, or lost souls are low energy level, addictive behavior, difficulties concentrating, tendency to have accidents, great financial problems, bad health, negative thoughts, or negative comments about God or angels.

There are many examples in the Bible which show clear evidence that the casting out of unclear energies, devils, and demons was a part of the healing work Jesus did. In Mark 1:39 (Authorized (King James) Version), you can read about Jesus: "And he preached in their synagogues throughout all Galilee, and cast out devils." In Luke 8:27-33 (AV), we can find the story of a sick man who was possessed by legions of devils and was healed by Jesus: "Then went the devils out of the man, and entered into the swine; and the herd ran violently down a steep place into the lake, and were choked." In Matthew 10:1 (AV) you can read: "And when he called unto him his twelve disciples, he gave them power against unclean spirits, to cast them out, and to heal all manner of sickness and all manners of disease."

Before we start doing any healing work or communicate with the angels, we need to understand the invisible world of energy.

Clinging, Disoriented Souls and Beings

If a soul leaves the physical body (which most people call death) in a state of depression or shock, the energetic frequency of this soul is very low and it is difficult for the soul to remember how to find the light. I call these souls disoriented souls. Some souls have unfinished business, usually involving family members, friends, or even their own murderer. The TV series *Ghost Whisperer* and *Medium* are based on this phenomenon. The story lines might be fictional, but it is a fact that earthbound and disoriented souls exist everywhere.

Earthbound spirits contact me since they know I can help them find their way into the light. This can happen

in daily situations like grocery shopping. I remember
once going down the bread aisle in a supermarket with
my husband. Suddenly a loaf of bread fell down from
the shelf, without me or my husband touching it. Immediately, I could feel the presence of a spirit and I started
talking to it. I asked the spirit to prove its presence to
me with a sign. Not even a second later, another loaf of
bread catapulted from the shelf within a short distance
from me. There were no other customers around. My
husband had already left the aisle; he preferred to let
me take care of business and had gone off shopping. I
called upon Jesus, said a prayer, and helped the lost and
angry spirit find the light. The energy in the bread aisle
felt much lighter and peaceful afterwards. I am clairau-
dient and heard a little "thank you" from my angels. I
knew that the spirit had found the light. Helping earthbound spirits to transition is one of many important tools
that lightworkers need to know. Lightworkers are loving
people who want to help others, either through spiritual
healing, counseling, or teaching. Their main focus is
to be of service to humanity and all living beings. They
behave like angels on earth and help to fulfil the divine
plan of creating heaven on earth.

If you were attracted to this book and are dedicated
to doing the exercises and meditations suggested here,
the likelihood that you are a lightworker is nearly 100
percent.

Some decades ago, during my early studies of the
impact of energy on the health of humans and animals, I
attended a training and certification program at the Institute of Geopathology in Ahnatal, near Kassel, Germany.
This institute was founded by an engineer who taught
me a lot about dowsing, energetic grid structures of the
earth, the impact of elektrosmog, energy attachments,

passed life regressions, angel healings, and much more. To this day, I am grateful for his teachings about the fascinating world of energy which has had so much impact on people's lives, health, and happiness. I learned that the environment of a person has a huge effect on his or her ability to heal.

People are not sick because they inherited bad genes from their parents; genes just have the potential to be activated or not. The fascinating science of epigenetics explains how nongenetic factors, e.g., the energy of the environment, cause an organism's genes to behave (or express themselves) in different ways. I will refer to epigenetics, especially the work of Dr. Bruce Lipton, later on in chapter 9.

In the context of disoriented souls, I would like to point out so-called negative cosmic points. These points are locations where disoriented souls and beings of low vibration prefer to hang out. People who have a negative cosmic point in their bedroom are often aggressive, depressed, or have nightmares. If you have the suspicion that your bedroom is such a point or haunted, you should work with an expert who specializes in energetic clearing. You can also ask Archangel Michael for guidance, protection, and healing. Surround yourself with his beautiful energy while you sleep.

There is always a cause or reason for all energetic imbalances and disturbances. In some cases, it is not possible to remove a negative cosmic point or close an energy portal through which spirits can enter into our dimension. In these cases, I highly suggest you learn as much as you can about spirits since there always is a reason why you have the experience of their presence. Since you cannot "fix" this, it's better to move out. However, it is always important to identify the real cause of a problem or illness, and ideally transform those energies with the help of the angels.

The souls of deceased animals can also attach to the energy field of a person. I know of many cases where pets stayed with their owner and within their former environment after they passed on. They absorb some energy, but mainly want to continue to share their love. I have not seen an animal's soul be a cause for an illness.

Disoriented souls attach themselves for many different reasons; any person could be a host for them. Please do not think, "That can't happen to me." Every person should clear their energy field to stay vital and healthy.

Prepare for Meditation

Begin every meditation with a preparatory base meditation. Choose a place to do it in which you cannot be disturbed or interrupted. Attach a "do not disturb" sign to your door and turn off the phone. The place in which you meditate should be pleasant for you. Ideally, it will be a bright, tidy space, with only a few pieces of furniture and maybe a few angel pictures. If you like, you can place fresh flowers in the room, play quiet meditation music, and light incense or candles. Find your own ritual for feeling good and the time of day that is best for you, for example, directly after waking up in the morning or immediately before going to bed. If no extra room is available to you, a corner of your bedroom is also sufficient. You can also search for a nice place in nature if the weather is suitable.

It is important that the place elected by you is used primarily for meditating. With time, an energy field with higher and finer oscillations will form there and support your meditation positively. Make yourself at home in your special place. You can sit either upright if you tend to fall asleep during meditation, or simply lie down. Allow your arms to rest next to your body and make sure that no garment disturbs or restricts you. Close your eyes and inhale and exhale several times very deeply. While inhaling through the nose, feel how fresh air penetrates your lungs. Imagine that the inhaled air looks like white light and it fills your body, bit by bit, and completely cleanses it. Hold your breath about three seconds or longer, and breathe out through your mouth. While breathing out through your mouth, blow out all tension and stress from your body. Relax your arms and legs—every single finger and muscle—and let go of all everyday worries. Imagine that your whole head is emptied, while you simply pull the stopper, like from a bathtub. And like old bathwater, your anxious thoughts flow out of your head. Feel yourself relax more and more. With deep exhalations, dammed up emotions and fears will leave your body.

You can deepen this meditation with the Angel Breath, which I will explain in the next chapter. Then begin with the following main meditation.

Meditation to Remove Disoriented Souls and Entities

First, direct your consciousness upon your internal divine flame or divine spring. Visualize this as a pure golden-white light which is in the center of your body; it looks like a beaming, bright star. See with your spiritual eye how the bright light from the center of the body extends with every breath. After repeatedly breathing in and out, the light fills your whole body and extends on and on, until it reaches the borders of the physical body. Then it extends into your whole body system—your emotional body, your mental body, and your spiritual body—until it reaches a diameter between eight and fifteen feet. The extended light forms a big light column which, in the end, reaches down to the center of the earth and up to the center of the universe.

Now ask Jesus Christ, Archangel Michael, and the assisting angels to show the disoriented souls and spirit beings the way to their paradise.

Paradise is not necessarily the realm of the light, because not all beings want to go to the light. Many fear it because they think they will be punished. Those beings just want to go to a place where they feel fine and which corresponds to their images of paradise. Do not make the mistake of prescribing your paradise to other souls, but leave it to Jesus Christ and the angels to lead away those souls and spirit beings. The column of light which you have built up serves merely as an energetic lift.

Concentrate further upon this column of light and inhale divine light deeply from the divine source. Maybe you have to yawn without being tired, and maybe even tears run down your cheeks without feeling sadness or other emotions. This process can last from ten to twenty minutes.

Make sure that all souls are removed from your aura and the column of light. If fearing souls cling to you, open your heart a little bit further and send out love and compassion. Ask the angels to dissolve the fear of these souls and to extinguish the reason they hold on to you or the place you are. Then, they can also be led away.[1]

---

1. In case there are very stubborn occupants, so-called powers of the darkness, who do not want to go away or always return, please see a professional expert who is specialized in energetic clearing. There can be numerous reasons for such entity attachments, for example, curses, magic attacks, or other karmic bonds caused in former incarnations.

Protective Energy Techniques

The best protection from energy attachments is raising the frequency of your own energy body (see also chapter 4). The energy body, also called the aura, is the immune system of the spiritual body.

If you cannot prevent that you have to go to an energetically contaminated place (hospital, underground station, airport, cemetery, etc.) or get in contact with an attacking angry person; you can apply the following visualization of white light:

Imagine that deep in your solar plexus a miniature sun or star glows—a beaming bright, white light. This sun or star shines throughout every cell of your physical body and, in addition, your energy body. It forms a cover of beaming white light which surrounds you fully and completely and protects you from all negative energies and entities.

If you are familiar with this technique, a quick thought is enough to activate the light cover. You can imagine that you switch on the light with an imaginary light switch, and you are protected immediately. This protective covering lasts approximately twelve hours and must be renewed regularly.

You can strengthen your protective shield, and also that of your clients, by calling forth the angels and asking them to enhance it with their angelic energy. For example, call upon Archangel Raphael and visualize beautiful green light permeating your energy body.

The Ascended Master Saint Germain, who is certainly well-known to some readers, offers us the opportunity to visualize a violet flame and transform dark energies into light with his help. Violet light protects against negativity and unwanted entities. At the same time, it can also transform and transmute negative energies that might already be attached to you. With pink light, you can also build up a protective shield, for example, with the intention that only love can penetrate your energetic shield.

Always be clear about your intention and call upon your guardian angels. Ask for divine protection as well as a legion of angels who will accompany you or your clients at all times. You can connect this practice with a prayer in your own words, depending on your faith and religion.

Etheric Cords

If you have feelings of fear, guilt, revenge, or grief concerning certain persons, you may feel as if you lead these people by an energetic leash, called an etheric cord. Etheric cords, which often are sent out unconsciously, connect you with other people and cause mutual energetic influencing. The longer and more intense this connection is, the thicker and stronger the cords become. Some cords look like the black hoses at a gas station. Beings that have attached themselves to you suck your life force through these energy tubes, as if they want to fill up their own gas tank for free.

Parents, siblings, life partners, children, and friends are the ones that we usually are connected to with energetic cords. Here, we are not talking about a beautiful love connection, but energetically draining or poisoning etheric cords.

People who work in supporting occupations, like healers, doctors, nurses, teachers, and advisers, often have many energetic cords which negatively connect them with their patients, pupils, and clients.

Through the connecting tubes, energy can flow back and forth. Since in this case no loving energy is exchanged, it is obvious what happens. If the person with whom you are connected etherically is furious and aggressive, this energy flows unfiltered into your own system and has toxic effects. If so-called energetic vampires tap your life force energy, you feel tired, depressed, and weak; you can even become seriously ill.

If you feel exhausted, lethargic, or worn out without much reason, and even feel physical pain (for example, back pains or headaches), you should definitely disconnect all etheric cords and dissolve the reason why they were there. It is very likely that you are influenced by them in a negative way.

Healers, doctors, nurses, therapists, and advisers should disconnect energetically after every treatment, every consultation, and/or conversation (including phone conversations) with patients or clients. If people feel guilty about something, they can easily be tapped. Subconsciously, they allow the attachments to pay energetically for their guilt. If people cannot forgive, they are automatically attached to a person, or even a deceased love one. They then have an "energetic leakage" through which they lose their life force energy.

Recently, I explained the meaning and consequences of etheric cords to my friend Kathrin. For a long time, she had been suffering from shoulder and back pain, and had headaches on a regular basis. I instructed her to do a cord cutting and QAH exercise with Archangel Michael.

After our conversation, she connected with Archangel Michael every day and practiced the following exercise. Six weeks later, when we talked again, she told me about her experiences.

"At the beginning, I perceived that the etheric cords were wrapped around my whole body like a mummy. I did the exercise every day during my walks in the garden. In the beginning, it seemed to me as if I could only take small steps because of the cords around my ankles. Archangel Michael cut the etheric cords every day. He first cut the ones around my feet, then the ones around my neck, and, in the end, the thick ones in my back.

"As you instructed me to do, I also asked Archangel Michael not only to cut those cords, but to do Quantum Angel Healing on me. As you said he would, he transformed the energetic reason the cords were there to begin with. He helped me alter my negative feelings, thoughts, belief systems, patterns, and my victim program.[2] From day to day, I felt freer. My thinking and feelings changed. My pain disappeared, and I felt that I had more and more energy. I could truly feel the intense healing and the big shift within myself afterward."

Kathrin also told me about the changes which had taken place in her relationship with her boyfriend, Frank. I already knew that Frank had not worked for ten years, had no income, and lived in her house for free. Kathrin was a hard-working woman who financially took care of both of them. As a consequence of her energy work with Archangel Michael, Kathrin not only cut her etheric cords, but changed internally; her transformation had a major impact on her relationship with Frank. She felt so much freer and better about herself that Frank became worried. He felt uncomfortable enough around his empowered girlfriend to make some positive life changes for himself.

He did not know anything about Kathrin's Quantum Angel Healing work, but he perceived an inexplicable

---

2. Victim program discussed later in chapter 10.

change in her. After five weeks, he told Kathrin that he no longer could continue the unbalanced relationship as it was. Frank's declaration was like a miracle to her. For the first time in ten years, Frank looked for a job and started working shortly after that. Kathrin's long-desired wish had come true, and from then on, her relationship with Frank developed very positively. It felt to her like she was dating a new person, one who was able to take her out to dinner and with whom she could share some quality time.

We also have etheric cords to former friends and, especially, those with whom we've had intimate relationships. Energetic connections exist until we cut the cords and consciously transform these energies. Etheric cords are very often the reason why people cannot find a new partner after a separation, or why they are simply unable to move on.

The strong impact of etheric cords can clearly be seen in Lisa's example. Lisa is a smart, good-looking beautician. She thought her relationship with her boyfriend, David, was finally over after five years. Lisa had left David three times before, always for a good reason: he had cheated on her with a different woman each time. In the past, she had been willing to get back with him after a short time apart and some sort of apology.

When Lisa came to see me, the last breakup had been four months before, but she still thought of David daily, even though she had not seen or heard from him. "Does he not miss me at all? Did he not love me?" she asked me. These were the tantalizing questions which brought sleepless nights to her.

During my treatment with Lisa, I discovered that she had a thick, black energy cord attached to her heart chakra, and another one attached to her base chakra, through which she was connected to David. Every time she thought of him, she felt pain in her heart; she was unable to date another man. After Archangel Michael cut the energetic cords and deep transformational Quantum Angel Healing—that went all the way back to her childhood—took place, Lisa felt better immediately. She slept through the night for the first time after the breakup and did not think about David the next day.

The day after our treatment, Lisa's phone rang. David called, supposedly just to say hello and to see how she was doing. This was not a coincidence but is rather typical after a successful energetic separation and healing. People who have drained your energy immediately feel that a change has taken place after you've undergone treatment, and, in many cases, they would like to reattach themselves to you. Without Quantum Angel Healing and energy transformation, it is easy for these cords to form again. All this happens between people without them being aware of it. The only exception to this is "the ones who are in the know"; these are the people that often live off other people's energy intentionally. This is very common in work-related relationships.

Lisa learned a lot during her time apart from David and was able to transform her old patterns and programs. Her old "love hurts program" (chapter 13) was released from her being and she was able to really forgive David. Their old relationship drama was no longer possible, since David had also shifted and healed his past. A year later, the couple moved to Maui.

Cutting the Cords and Protection from Archangel Michael

Start again with the preparatory base meditation (see page 31), until you are completely relaxed. Then connect with Archangel Michael through the Angel Breath (chapter 4); it should happen instantaneously. Feel his energy surround you, and get even more comfortable in his presence. He has a sword of bright blue light with which he can cut all negative energetic connections. (If you have difficulties visualizing a sword of light, simply imagine the light sabers of the Jedi Knights in the *Star Wars* movies.)

The presence of Archangel Michael makes you feel protected and safe. You can ask for his help in your own words, for example, "Archangel Michael, I need your help. Please come with your sword of light and cut all negative energetic connections with persons, situations, places, and objects that are harmful for me and/or rob me of my life force energy. Conduct a Quantum Angel Healing on me and seal my energy field so that a renewed harmful connection is not possible."

Imagine Archangel Michael sealing your body and your aura with thick, golden-white energy foam, which is impenetrable for any form of negative energy. Only love can permeate it.

You can also ask the archangel to specifically cut any negative etheric cords with certain people, for example, your father, your mother, your brother or sister, or your ex-partner or ex-spouse. You can ask that their awareness be increased, so that they too can see behind the curtain of illusions and realize their own connection to the divine source.

It is very important that you also ask for a deep transformational QAH after the cord cutting. This step has a profound impact on your relationship and karmic connection with the specific person. QAH, and with it energy transformation, takes place on all levels and dimensions of our being, in all directions of time and space. This will be explained in detail in chapter 14 when I explain the Angelic Healing Formula.

It is very likely that people can physically feel when the etheric cords have been cut and the energy released. Some people's postures improve immediately. I remember a client who had severe scoliosis. During an energy treatment with the angels, I had my hands on the client's back. A lot of energy was flowing. Archangel Michael cut the energy cords and deep healing took place. All of a sudden, I felt a strong quiver underneath my hands. I looked at the client's back and saw it straightening out in front of my eyes.

Taking Salt Baths to Cleanse Your Aura

A Dead Sea salt bath is very healing. It is a powerful way to help you release psychic and physical toxins. Cleansing and clearing is also the best way to enhance your abilities to connect with your higher self, the angels, and the spirit world.

The Dead Sea is located adjacent to Khirbet Qumran, Israel, a home base for the ancient mystical Jewish group known as the Essenes. The Essenes are known for their spiritual healing and manifestation knowledge. Their knowledge was found in the Dead Sea Scrolls, which numerous experts consider to be the lost book of the Bible. Jesus spent his youth studying with the Essenes.

The Dead Sea is about ten times saltier than the ocean, and its salt contains twenty-one minerals. Its water also has fifteen times more magnesium and fifty times more bromine than ocean water. Magnesium and bromine are both relaxing agents, so soaking in a bath filled with Dead Sea salt promotes relaxation. The high mineral content of Dead Sea salts also softens your skin. Salt draws toxins out of your pores, because the water breaks the salt's molecules apart (NaCl separates into Na and Cl). This conducts the salt's electrons faster, which energetically clears and massages you. Purchase Dead Sea salts in health food stores or online from various sources. Be sure that your bath salts are all natural, without artificial ingredients.

Important: Please use Dead Sea salts and not any other kind of bath salts!

How to take a bath with Dead Sea salts:

- Fill your bathtub with warm water and pour a pound of Dead Sea salts into the water. The warmer and saltier your bath, the greater the effect. You can add natural, organic bubble bath if you like.

- Enjoy your bath and soak for about twenty minutes. Make sure that you turn onto your stomach to cleanse your throat and heart chakra. Dip your head under the water a few times to cleanse the chakras of the ear, third eye, and crown.

- Drain the water from your tub. Rinse off the salt and relax.

Afterward, you will feel energized and cleansed. The best time for your baths is the early morning or early evening. You will feel relaxed for many hours. This method is very effective for cleansing your aura, and you can apply it on a regular basis—daily when required.

Energy Techniques to Cleanse Your Home and Work Environment

The energetic cleansings of your home and workplace are as important as the methods for personal cleansing that I have explained above. How often you need to clear your home depends on what is happening there and how often you have people visiting and bringing their "stuff" over to your place. If you have many people visiting your practice or meditation facilities, it is important to do a clearing on a regular basis. Whatever clearing method you prefer, always include your angels and spiritual helpers in the ceremony.

Smudging

Sage, cedar, copal, and sweetgrass are sacred herbs collected and burned by the shamans of North America. The burning of the herbs is called "smudging." The use of herbs is as ancient as the use of fire. As the shamans learned to control fire, they found that certain plants and resins, when burned, produced magical benefits, such as visions of past, present, and future events; attracted beneficial spirits; removed negative elements and forces; and promoted physical and spiritual healing. Burning white sage drives out bad spirits, feelings, energies, and influences. It also keeps unwanted spirits from entering the area where a cleansing took place.

- Before you start the smudging, prepare by opening all windows and doors—including closet, cabinet, and storage room doors. This way the smoke can enter all of the spaces of the home or facility.

- Call forth your angels and spirit guides with a prayer and the Angel Breath. Set the intention that the smoke is blessed and that your place is cleared from any disturbing or harmful energies and entities.

- Take a handful of sage and put it in a nonflammable bowl, dish, or abalone shell. Light the sage and blow out the flame after it gets going, then blow into the smoldering embers. If it burns out, just relight it and keep going.

- First smudge yourself starting with the bottoms of your feet. Then work the smoke up around your body and around your head and crown chakra. After that is done, start at a doorway and direct the smoke completely around the door frame. You will repeat this in every room starting at the doorway to each room and moving to the exterior doors to the apartment or house. To help direct the smoke into drawers and closets, you can either fan a feather, if you have one, or your hand. The idea is to let the smudge smoke get into and around everything within the home or workspace.

- When you have completed every room, say another prayer, thanking God, the angels, and your spirit guides for their help and blessings, and asking that the smoke carries away all negative entities and energies from your home or workspace. Through the open windows and doors, the smoke will be purged from the interior and fresh air and chi will flow back into your living or workspace.

- After closing the windows and doors, sit down and relax for a while and begin to enjoy your cleansed environment. You can also burn some fragrant incense, candles, or sweetgrass. The pleasant smell invites good spirits into your home and covers the pot-like smelling sage.

- You may notice the difference of energy right away or especially the next day, as will visitors who come to your home or workspace.

The Burning Pot

One of my favorite cleansing methods is the so-called burning pot, which I learned about from Dr. Joshua David Stone. Just like you need special detergent for certain stains in your clothes, there are certain cleansing techniques you need for energies that will not leave easily, even when you smudge the place. From my experience, the burning pot has always been the most thorough method of clearing on all energetic levels. If you have a large house, I recommend doing this clearing ceremony in every room. In a small apartment, simply put it in the center of the living space.

For about five minutes, the pot will burn up all the etheric, astral, and mental energies in the room. Here are the steps:

- Open all windows and doors—including closet, cabinet, and storage room doors. Be careful not to create a draft in the room.

- Call forth your angels and spirit guides with a prayer and the Angel Breath. Set the intention that this ceremony is blessed and that your place is cleared from any disturbing or harmful energies and entities.

- Put a nonflammable plate in the center of the room, and place a small metal pot on top of it. In the pot, pour a half inch of Epsom salts.

- When you want to begin the clearing ceremony, pour no more than an inch of rubbing alcohol over the Epsom salts and throw a burning match into the rubbing alcohol.

- Pay attention! The flames can burn high and twirl around, almost like a powerful tiny tornado in the burning pot.[3]

- Depending on the energies that are burned up and transformed, you might see different colors or even different shapes in the burning flames.

- After the flames have burned down, the fire will extinguish itself. This means that the cleansing ceremony has ended.

- Thank God, your angels, and your spirit guides for their help and ask them for further protection of your home or workspace.

- After closing the windows and doors, sit down and relax for a while and begin to enjoy your cleansed environment, or continue the ceremony in other rooms of the house.

- After you are done, you will feel the crisp and clear energy of the rooms immediately.

---

3. Because you are working with an open fire, you need to take precautions, such as having a fire extinguisher at hand, in case of an accident.

You can repeat this cleansing ceremony as often as you like. For teaching and healing facilities, I recommend a burning pot before starting an event. After the event is over, I recommend a clearing meditation.

Saltwater

If you work with more than one client per day, I recommend placing a medium-sized bowl with saltwater (approximately five tablespoons of Dead Sea salt) either underneath your massage table or in the right corner of your practice room.

Ask Archangel Michael and his helpers to watch over energies and entities that might be released during a treatment. If they cannot be transformed right away, they can be caught in the saltwater. Don't be surprised if the water turns dark or brownish; that indicates a strong release of negative energies. Please refresh the saltwater after each client, and pour the water into the toilet. It is not suitable for watering your plants or garden!

Releasing Old Energies

Even if we all walk our very personal spiritual path and have different religious backgrounds, there are certain milestones that each of us has to pass. One important milestone or initiation is learning to let go. Only if we let go of old emotions, energies, environments, and people that no longer serve us, can we create the necessary space for spiritual growth and new, important things and people in our life.

Many of my clients long for change and new things: a new job, a new partner, a new home, etc. It used to be that things did not change for decades and people asked, "How can I change my life?" The high energies of the new age around 2012 and beyond will make people change their current life situations, whether they are open to it or not. It is necessary to just take the next step of evolution at this point in time. There are three things I would like to bring to your awareness:

- If you want to change or change is happening in your life, old patterns and programs work against you.

- Change will not come easily if you hold on to old energies, emotions, people, and environments that no longer support the new you.

- It is also of great importance to transform fears of change that keep you in a fear-based matrix.

One of the greatest fears is the fear of change. This fear includes fear of new environments, new relationships, and new things that you have never done before. You are not alone with this; even dolphins, who are very intelligent beings, feel the same way about change. You have probably heard about swimming with dolphins as a tourist attraction or for healing purposes. Swimming with dolphins is usually offered in a controlled environment, where the dolphins live within a gated area of the ocean. Tourists can touch them, feed them, and hold on to them while swimming, which is a lot of fun. Even if you opened the gate to the ocean, the dolphins, who are used to being in captivity, would not swim away. They are afraid of change and unfamiliar terrain, just like humans. Their internal programming is stronger than their wish to be free. Does that sound familiar to you?

Take a moment to think about your habits in your daily life. Do you notice that you always buy the same groceries in the same store? That you have your favorite meals, restaurants, TV shows, clothes, pillows and blankets, etc.? These habits reveal the subconscious programs that make you do certain things every day. They become habits—sometimes addictions—and are not at all a conscious choice.

We all are rooted in a familiar family or work environment. The longer we are in the same situation, the stronger our roots and attachments are to it. Just imagine uprooting an old, big tree which has been standing in the same place for decades. Imagine its deep roots and you will get an idea of how difficult that might be. Through events like divorce and unemployment, people are uprooted all the time. This causes enormous pain and damage to our energy fields, which often is the cause for later physical illnesses. This is also true for sudden withdrawal from long-term use of drugs or alcohol. In order to really heal a life change, it is necessary to remove old roots completely and heal the energy and/or physical body. This is important to know, especially in the new time of change.

During a Quantum Angel Healing, all attaching roots are removed. Patterns and programs are transformed, belief systems and limiting emotions are changed, and possible wounds are healed. The chakra system and the whole energy field look bright and clear. New light-filled life-force energy can flow into the DNA and activate your true potential.

If you want to prepare for the coming changes in your life, start today. You can start in your home and clear out cluttered closets, drawers, basements, and storage spaces, including the attic and garage. Throw away old shoes, clothes that you have not worn for many years, books, paperwork, inherited memorabilia, and gifts that have no meaning to you. All these things carry a specific

Eva-Maria Mora

vibration; if they are previously owned, they have the
energetic imprint of the former owner.

Go and shop in different stores, eat foods you have
never tasted before, get a new haircut, and do things that
you have never done before. If you start this process of
change, you create room for new beginnings, and new
energies will flow into your life.

If you feel resistance and have a hard time letting go
of things, please consider the following story:

A tourist traveled with a big backpack and spent the
night in a cloister. He wondered about the sparse and
poor-looking place and asked the monk, "Where do you
have your furniture?" The monk looked at him and asked
back, "Where do you have your furniture?"

"My furniture?" the tourist asked, thinking he had
not heard right. "I am only passing through here."

"Exactly," answered the monk, "and so are we."

My client, Jennifer, went through a painful divorce
and lived a single life for about three years. She came to
me for an appointment because she felt lonely and wanted
to have a new life partner. Jennifer was a very attractive
woman with dark curly hair and beautiful brown eyes.
She could not understand why no man seemed to be
interested in her. She was wearing an exquisite, valuable
pearl necklace with large, shiny pearls when she came to
see me. During our QAH treatment, the angels pointed
out to me that there was a distinct energetic pattern and
belief system attached to the pearls. I asked Jennifer to
tell me more about the necklace. She told me that it was
a gift from her ex-husband; he had given it to her for
their first wedding anniversary. It was the only valuable
piece that remained in her possession after a marriage
of seven years. The angels recommended that she take

off the necklace, even though it was beautiful; it carried strong energies from her ex-husband.

The memories from her marriage that were attached to the pearl necklace were blocking Jennifer's heart chakra. The signal that she was sending out from her heart, "I am interested in a new relationship," was disturbed by the signal from the necklace, which was, "I am a married woman and my husband gives me beautiful gifts." Her heart chakra was blocked by these conflicting energies. Without being aware of it, Jennifer was sending out confusing signals. This is the reason why she could not attract a new life partner. The angels advised her to take off the necklace and give it away. Jennifer stared at me as I told her this. "Give it away?" she asked doubtfully with her eyes wide open. I explained to her that by taking money for it, she would only exchange the form of the same energy that was given to her by her ex-husband. Finally she understood and decided to donate the necklace to her church which had a big charity event. A young man saw the necklace and bought it at a very reasonable price for his bride. He was so excited about this opportunity that he invited Jennifer to his wedding. She went to the wedding, which was a few weeks later, and met a very handsome man who became her husband a year later.

This story shows how a change in energy can become a life change. During the many years of my work, thousands of clients and students were able to apply energy clearing and QAH techniques to change their lives for the better. A very important technique and essential part of QAH is the Angel Breath, which I explain in the next chapter.

CHAPTER 4

Healing in Communication
with the Angels

What is the wisdom of a book compared to the wisdom
of an angel?
                    —*Friedrich Hölderlin, German poet (1770–1843)*

The angels have told me that intensive breathing is the
simplest method you can use to increase your own frequency. Your breath cleanses your energy channel, which
functions like a chimney, and the additional oxygen facil-
itates the transportation of information into your cells.
Blood is fed with oxygen via the respiratory organs, and
your circulation then distributes this oxygen throughout
your organism. The capacity of your body's transportation
channels, and the quality of the materials delivered—for
example the neuropeptides, including the energy and
information that accompanies them—are crucial to your
body's health and the energy level of all its cells.

I believe the key prerequisite for the health of the
entire body is optimal communication between all cells
and organs. If this communication is impaired, misunderstandings and supply bottlenecks occur, and this triggers
chain reactions that upset your physical and energy bal-

ance. I believe suppressed emotions and unconscious programs are the main cause of disturbed communication. However good your intentions for maintaining your health are, such emotions and programs will always cause "error messages" in your organism if they are not released (pages 150 ff. describes this in greater detail).

Our lungs are not only air filters; they are also filters for information. With the right intention and appropriate energy, disrupted communication within our bodies can be resolved through breathing.

The effects of intensive breathing are amazing. By dissolving old energies—combined with intention, Angel Breath, and the transmission of angel energy—you can cleanse the human energy field, eliminate free radicals, release psychic and energy blocks, and watch apparently chronic diseases literally vanish before your eyes.

Angel Breath

Angel Breath

1. Relax by breathing in and out slowly three to four times. Breathe in through the nose and out through the mouth. Empty your head completely; let go of all your thoughts. Relax all your muscles.

2. Imagine that the air you are breathing consists of many tiny, white light molecules. These light molecules, which look like little bottle brushes with bright, shining bristles, race through your energy channels and clean them.

3. Now slowly bring your palms together. When there is only about four to five inches between your hands, you will clearly feel a little resistance, a ball of energy the size of an orange. Let this ball of energy circulate playfully between your hands. *Let your breath and your thoughts follow the ball of energy.*

4. When you breathe in the next time, inhale the ball of energy into your solar plexus (at your navel) with the power of your imagination.

5. Then, with the next exhalation, let the ball of energy wander down the lower half of your body and to the center of the earth. There, it is transformed again and energized with all the minerals, vitamins, trace elements, and energies that your body needs.

6. Now inhale again. Like a tree that draws up its nutrients from the earth, you imbibe the ball of energy from the earth with your breath. During this inhalation, the transformed ball of energy quickly moves up through your entire body—or rather your energy channel.

7. When the ball of energy reaches your head, breathe out and feel how it flies through your crown chakra to the center of the universe, to the source of divine energy. There, it is energized with divine energy.

8. When you breathe in this ball of energy again, ask God to add the angel energy to it that will be of the greatest help to you and/or the treatment of your client. You can address any angels you know directly by their name.

9. Breathe out, imagining how the angel energies flow through your energy channel as bright white or colored rays of light, and emerge from your hands.

10. Notice that many angels are surrounding you, treating your client.

Repeat steps 4 through 10 twice, and as you do this, imagine that the ball of energy becomes larger and larger, and extends at least two to three meters beyond your physical body. Notice how the angel energy forms take shape. Like a genie emerging from a bottle, whose energy can take on various forms, the angels can also take on multiple appearances.

Now notice how one or several angels lay their hands on you, and how this generates an even more intensive energy field. Let go of this image. During the entire treatment, breathe as described above. The ball of energy (your breath) will move regularly through you from the center of the earth to the divine source and then emerge from your hands again. Regulate the intensity of your breathing as you wish. Let your breath flow in and out naturally at your own pace, and make sure you can really feel the energy flowing out of your hands when you exhale.

Only when the energy is flowing from your hands should you put them on your client's body.

Now your Angel Antenna is switched on. You will feel how the angel energies are flowing through your energy channel. You will be able to receive messages and transmit healing energies. Relax and develop a feeling for the angel energies. Keep up the Angel Breath during the entire treatment, and firmly hold your intention throughout.

Treating Physical Pain

1. If your client has physical pain, lightly and care-
    fully lay your hands on the place that hurts. Relax
    your hands and imagine the bright ball of energy
    between them. The energy will flow between your
    hands, and flow through the part of the body/organ
    that hurts from both sides. By placing your palms
    on the painful area and having the ball of energy
    surround it, you create a strong field of resonance.
    The energy in the organ/cells will increase.

2. Ask your client how intense the pain is, or what
    he/she is feeling. Ask him/her to rate the intensity
    of pain on a scale from one to ten. Ten designates
    the most intense level of pain and one the least.
    Test the area after five minutes, and then again
    after ten, to see whether the pain has lessened,
    and what the client is feeling. Leave your hands
    in one place for ten to fifteen minutes.

3. Ask the angels to heal the cause of the pain, and pay
    attention as you do this to any images or messages
    you receive. Communicate them to your client, and
    ask him/her to tell you what he/she may be expe-
    riencing. (Work on eradicating emotional causes
    and beliefs. For further details, see below.)

4. If the pain moves or changes, follow your intu-
    ition and the guidance of the angels, and go to
    another place with your hands. If you feel that
    the energy vibration of the place you are treat-
    ing has adapted to the quality of energy in your
    hands (i.e., the vibrational level is the same), you
    can end the treatment.

One of my clients, Lisa, was fifty-one years old and had severe problems with her left hip. Sometimes she could barely walk due to the pain. Her energy treatment went well, and after ten minutes she was free of pain. The angels worked with a lot of green and golden light; Lisa was able to describe exactly what they were doing. She saw spirals of light circling around her whole body, although my hands remained on her hips the whole time. During the treatment I received the message, "three years old." As always, I trusted the angels fully, pushing aside any contrary experience or images of my own. I personally have no memories from when I was three, but I asked, "Lisa, can you remember what happened in your life when you were three?" She immediately broke into tears. Sobbing, she told me, "Of course I remember! On my third birthday, my mother was in the hospital giving birth to my sister. No one had time for me on that special day. My father was also at the hospital, and a neighbor looked after me. I didn't get any presents, and the baby was the center of all the attention."

This emotional pain from Lisa's third birthday was still stuck in her energy body, and had caused the pain in her hip. The angels continued to work, guided her through a tailor-made visualization, and Lisa was able to finally forgive her sister and her parents. The energy block was released, and Lisa was free of pain from then on.

Treating Emotional Pain and Blockages

As the previous case illustrated, the energy of suppressed emotions and psychic suffering often leads to physical problems (see also part 2 of this book). This makes it vital to transform this energy before it can cause disease in the physical body.

1. Lay your hands lightly and carefully on the front and back of your client's heart chakra. Your touch should be very gentle. Relax your hands, imagining a bright ball of energy between your hands the entire time. The energy will flow back and forth between your hands, and through the heart chakra.

2. Now imagine your client's heart chakra opening, and how the painful, blocked emotions are released (tears will often flow at this point), and how the angels clean the chakra and fill it with bright, loving angel energy.

3. Speak to your client about the images and messages you receive.

4. Check whether there are any disturbing energy connections. If so, release them.

5. Help your client forgive the person who caused their painful experience. Use visualizations and meditations guided by the angels.

6. Work in the same way with all the other chakras. Ask the respective angel for help, use the corresponding colors, and work through any themes that come up.

My client Peggy, who was thirty-two years old, did not have any physical complaints. On the surface, she was healthy. But beyond what was visible to others, she suffered great emotional pain buried deep in her heart.[1]

---

1. Be particularly careful with clients who say they do not have any problems!

I treated Peggy's heart chakra for about twenty minutes. Suddenly she felt compression and pain in her chest, and said, "I'm afraid. I feel as though I'm losing the ground from under my feet. I'm cold. I'd prefer to stop."

The angels encouraged me to continue, and I assured Peggy that her pent-up feelings would be released; this would all be for her own good. Peggy's heart chakra opened, and she broke into tears. She cried her heart out for the next ten minutes. The angels showed me baby images over and over again and said, "All is well. You are loved." I passed on this message to Peggy, and she sobbed even more. After she had gone through a whole packet of Kleenex, I treated her for another ten minutes. Finally, she calmed down and her whole body relaxed. She saw golden and green light, felt the presence of the angels, and sensed an inner peace she had never felt before.

It turned out that Peggy had been a premature baby. She had spent the first four months of her life in an incubator, without any real touch, and without any contact with her mother. She had had difficulties her whole life being touched and accepting love. Our session healed this trauma. Peggy went on to train as a Quantum Angel practitioner, and she now regularly visits premature babies at the hospital near her, conducting energy treatments for the infants.

Letting Go of/Replacing Fears and Limiting Belief Systems

We all know people who seem to have one problem after another. They've scarcely gotten over one illness before they come down with another. What's important is to heal the underlying emotions and transform the causative thought patterns and programs; otherwise, they will simply lead to a new emotional hurt or physical disease.

1. First, have a preliminary discussion with your client to find out about any limiting belief systems and programs they may have.

2. Put your hands lightly and carefully on both sides of your client's head, above their temples. Your touch should be very gentle. Relax your hands and imagine a bright ball of energy between them.

3. Visualize the angels unzipping an imaginary golden zipper on your client's head, and removing all the limiting beliefs and programs responsible for your client's problem. Your client will give permission for this by saying, "I release all the limiting beliefs and programs that have caused…"

4. The energies and information that now flow through your hands into the head of your client contain new beliefs, such as, "I am healthy. I am loved."

5. Zip up the imaginary zipper. Ask your client to visualize a positive self image (for example, that he/she is completely healthy), and ask him/her to say "I am free, I am free, I am free."

Claudia, a twenty-year-old client, sprained her right foot on a cycling tour with her boyfriend. She came hobbling into my practice, and was furious with her boyfriend because she believed he was responsible for her accident. In the preliminary discussion, it emerged that she had wanted to study medicine in Los Angeles, but her boyfriend was working in Phoenix and didn't want to move, so they argued constantly.

During the energy treatment, I received the message, "Mother," from the angels. Often, the angels don't speak in full sentences; they behave more like a prompter in the theater. They give you key words that are essential to the treatment. So I asked Claudia about her mother, and it turned out that Claudia's father had prevented her mother—a nurse—from working the night shift. He was a jealous man and accused her of secretly meeting other men. Claudia was repeating the pattern she had subconsciously adopted from her parents. During the treatment, the pain in her foot lessened, the swelling went down, and Claudia was able to release the old pattern.

Later, I learned that Claudia broke up with the boyfriend who so selfishly held her back. During medical school, she met a new boyfriend, a young doctor with a similar calling to help humanity.

CHAPTER 5

The Chakra System and the Angels

The word *chakra* literally means "wheel or circle." It is a Sanskrit word, and the verb *chakr* means "to shiver." Sanskrit is the ancient language of India in which most religious and spiritual literature was written. Chakras are, in fact, rotating wheels of energy. They spin and move energy up and down the body and play a critical role in keeping both your physical and energy bodies healthy.

Human beings have numerous chakras or focal points of energy. In this book, we will concentrate on the seven main chakras and their functions. These seven chakras are located in your energy body about six inches from your physical body. They run up the center of the body, parallel to the spinal column. Each chakra has a different frequency, color, and vibration. Some clairvoyant people can see the chakras and their different colors, but to most folks, they are invisible. You can compare the chakras to the propeller of an airplane, which becomes invisible when spinning very fast. The human chakras also spin very fast, which is why they become invisible to the human eye. If the chakra system functions properly, chakras spin in a clockwise direction.

All chakras absorb energies from around you and transmit these frequencies as subtle impulses to your nervous system, glandular system, and the organs of your physical body. They are the communicators within your system, transmitting and retaining lots of information. Every time you experience a situation or feel an emotion, the chakras record the energy of that experience and store it.

After a while, the chakras can get clogged and blocked, so it is important to cleanse and balance them; otherwise, you will feel tired, depressed, or even sick. If a chakra is clogged, it means that the flow of energy in the physical body is likewise limited. The chakra can't absorb new energy, and instead repels it. In the Indian tradition, the energy that flows between the first chakra (base chakra) and the seventh chakra (crown chakra) is called kundalini energy. In different yoga traditions, this flow of energy is enhanced by physical exercises and breathing techniques in order to achieve enlightenment. During these exercises you connect with the energies from the earth and the cosmos, just like you do with the Angel Breath.

In order for this stream of energy to flow, each chakra has to be clean and open. If only one of the chakras is closed, the balance between the flow of energy from the earth and the flow of energy from the cosmos is disturbed. This creates disharmony in your physical body and in your life.

Suppressed emotions can clog the different chakras, which will end up being deformed and blocked with stagnant energy. The spinning movement becomes unbalanced or is misdirected to turn counterclockwise. If this happens, the energy will leak outward and the metabolism of the physical body can't function properly or absorb much-needed new energies to this specific chakra. It can't absorb healing energies from the angels either, so the benefits from an energetic treatment are limited. In the worst case, a chakra can be completely filled with dense energies, unable to absorb any vital energy. In this case, we speak of a "closed chakra."

The Color Spectrum of the Chakra System

Although people can perceive the actual form of a chakra slightly differently (the most common perception is of a wheel or funnel), you'll find general agreement on their different colors. My experience is that depending on how clean or blocked a chakra is, the colors can be lighter or darker. Sometimes they even look muddy to me, and only after specific chakra clearings do they become lighter and more transparent again. The colors of the main seven chakras are like the colors of a rainbow, the so-called spectral colors of light. If you combine all the colors, you get pure, white light. The physical human body functions like a prism, which breaks the light as it flows through our energy channel. The different wavelengths of energy are perceived as different colors.

1. Base or root chakra   red

2. Sacral chakra   orange

3. Solar plexus chakra   yellow

4. Heart chakra   green (with pink)

5. Throat chakra   blue (pale) and greenish-blue

6. Third-eye chakra   dark blue and indigo

7. Crown chakra   violet, white, and golden

Since all colors flow together in the crown chakra and additional light energy flows into it from above, it might also appear to be white. When people are less light-filled, it looks more violet. White, bright light might radiate out of an open third-eye chakra so that its usual blue color appears only around its edges. This phenomenon can be found in many paintings of Indian gods and goddesses, who are usually portrayed as beings of light which have transformed their physical bodies and all earthly aspects.

Each chakra has a specific task regarding your physical and psychological health. In order to understand this healing method, it is important that you understand why chakra-clearing is relevant. It is simply the prerequisite to free-flowing communication and healing with angels. The frequencies transmitted by the angels can flow much more easily through a cleansed and open chakra system. The flowing energy activates the function of the system or energy channel, so the healing of the organs can take place. All organs correspond to the different chakras.

Before each Quantum Angel Healing treatment, the practitioner makes sure that his chakra system is cleansed and that the energies can flow freely. At the beginning of a session, he simply sets the intention for his hand chakras to open like a lid, which is removed from the center of the hand. Through the high-energy frequency that the QA practitioner maintains during a treatment, the client can entrain to this high vibration. With the help of the angels, stuck energies can be transformed and the chakras can be balanced. They will start spinning in the right direction, adjust to the optimal size (three to six inches in diameter), and align themselves in a straight line again.

Through the communication with the angels, a QAH practitioner can discern which energies, belief systems, and programs are causing problems for a client, and most importantly, how to transform them. The QAH practitioner puts his hands on the physical body, parallel to the chakra of the energy body and senses a possible blockage. If at any time during a treatment, a client feels that the energies are too intense, it might be because it's not what she or he is used to feeling, especially if the client's energy levels were low before the treatment. The QAH practitioner can assist the client by explaining that there can never be too much energy—it is never harmful. The client simply needs to breathe and relax, open up the feet chakras, and let energy flow out of his feet into the earth. A simple visualization, like that of pulling the stopper out of a bathtub in the center of the soles of the feet, will help to let the access energy flow out easily. If the client's knees should start hurting during a treatment, it usually indicates that the energies can't flow freely through the knee chakras. This can happen to clients who are inflexible or afraid of possible change. I call it the "fear of making the next step," and it can energetically block a knee chakra. Double check the flow of the Angel Breath and set your intention so that the healing energies can flow freely through your own energy channel and through your client's chakra system.

With regular chakra clearings, the crown chakra opens up, influencing all other chakras on the head in a positive way. This includes the ear chakras, which are located in the energy body above the ears. They radiate red and violet; if they are blocked, they look muddy and dark. Blocked chakras can also limit the communication with angels. A person with closed ear chakras is energetically "deaf" and can't receive the subtle frequencies of the angels. Limiting belief systems and subconscious fears, which I explained in chapter 1, can also prevent you from receiving the angels' information. You could be afraid to hear the voices of God and the angels, or to hear unpleasant information. To further develop clairaudience, it is also important to forgive people who have said something hurtful to you. Some people, for example, closed their ear chakras as children when they heard their parents arguing. They need to forgive their parents before they can fully open their ear chakras again.

The high-pitched ringing sound that many people hear from time to time is not tinnitus, but a sign that the ear chakras are opening and that they can receive the angels' frequencies, which can be translated into messages with some practice. Another phenomenon that is frequently misinterpreted is the opening of the heart chakra. Many people have closed up their heart chakras to protect themselves from emotional hurt. When this chakra opens, it can feel a little uncomfortable and is often mistaken for back pain. In each certification program, we have participants who notice a slight sore feeling in the back, right were the heart chakra is. They are relieved once they understand that it's an indication of the opening of the heart chakra, which was caused by the loving and light-filled work they did during exercises in class. This unusual feeling in the back disappears very quickly, especially after the heart healing meditation with Archangel Raphael, which we do during the four-day QAH certification program.

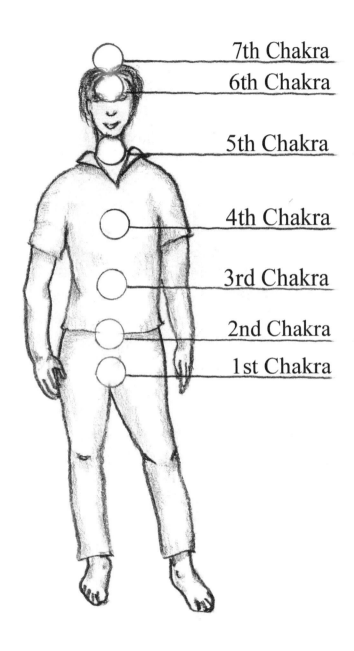

7th Chakra

6th Chakra

5th Chakra

4th Chakra

3rd Chakra

2nd Chakra

1st Chakra

The First Chakra

Name: Root chakra or base chakra (Sanskrit: Muladhara chakra)

Location: At the end of the spine, at the perineum near the anus

Related Glands: Adrenal glands and gonads (ovaries and testicles)

Responsible for: Large intestine, lower part of the small intestine, rectum, prostate, ovaries, testicles, urinary tract, bladder, uterus, coccyx, blood, marrow and cell construction, water household, and salt household (in case of pregnancy: placenta, umbilical cord, and fetus)

Effects of hypoactivity:

At the physical level: No interest in sex, difficulty reaching orgasm, higher likelihood of miscarriages, tendency to get infected with sexually transmitted diseases, irregular periods

At the emotional level: Lack of confidence, endurance, and determination; feeling unloved; fear of abandonment

Effects of hyperactivity:

At the physical level: Very strong sexual drive, increased adrenal hormone production

At the emotional level: Feeling self-centered, stingy, tyrannical, and arrogant

Effects of balanced activity: Centeredness, good stamina and health, unlimited physical energy

Theme: Career, finances, home, family, material security

Color: Red

Angel: Sandalphon

The Second Chakra

Name: Sacral chakra (Sanskrit: Svadhishthana chakra)

Location: Just below the navel, lower abdomen
Related glands: Adrenal glands
Responsible for: Adrenal glands, adrenalin level, blood sugar level, blood pressure, gonads, ovaries, prostate, testicles
Effects of hypoactivity:
At the physical level: Irregular kidney and spleen function, disturbance of sexual energy, impotence, infertility, inflammations of the ovaries, uterine carcinoma, endometriosis, low blood pressure
At the emotional level: Lethargy, tendency to repress feelings, tendency to hold on to others, tendency to feel guilty, coldness
Effects of hyperactivity:
At the physical level: Excessive sexual energy, indigestion, uterine or prostate cancer, high blood pressure
At the emotional level: Negativity, inhibitions
Effects of balanced activity: Friendliness, optimism, creativity, distinctive imagination
Theme: Addictions (drugs, alcohol, food, sex, etc.)
Color: Orange
Angel: Gabriel and Raphael

The Third Chakra

Name: Solar plexus chakra (Sanskrit: Manipura chakra)
Location: Above the navel and stomach area
Related glands: Pancreas
Responsible for: Pancreas, stomach, spleen, liver, gallbladder, nervous system, bones, lower back muscles
Effects of hypoactivity:
At the physical level: Low function of the metabolic organs, tendency to break bones, malfunctioning insulin production, weak nerves

At the emotional level: Depression, rejection, lack of trust, worries about what others think of you, fear of being alone, confusion, insensitivity to feel emotions

Effects of hyperactivity:

At the physical level: Diabetes, pancreatitis, soreness of lower back muscles, high-speed metabolism, nervous tension

At the emotional level: High temper, judgmental thoughts, workaholic attitude, perfectionism, demanding attitude, overemotionality, dissatisfaction with relationships, lack of connection between sexuality and love

Effects of balanced activity: Spontaneity, outgoing attitude, happiness, relaxation, self-respect, great personal strength, awareness of own gifts and talents

Theme: Power and control

Color: Yellow

Angel: Michael, Raphael, and Uriel

The Fourth Chakra

Name: Heart chakra (Sanskrit: Anahata chakra)

Location: At the center of the chest, at the level of the heart

Related glands: Thymus and parathyroid

Responsible for: Bones, muscle tissue, heart, lower lungs, blood pressure, blood circulation system

Effects of hypoactivity:

At the physical level: Heart rhythm disturbances, weak circulation, weak immune system

At the emotional level: Worries about self, depression, paranoia, indecision, fear of getting hurt, fear of letting go, abandonment issues, doubts, insecurity

Effects of hyperactivity:

At the physical level: Heart attack, pneumonia, psychic disturbances

At the emotional level: Tendency to act challenging, hyper-criticality, moodiness, melodrama, manic depression

Effects of balanced activity: Empathy, willingness to see the good in everyone, friendliness, open-mindedness, open-heartedness, participation in active social life

Theme: Interpersonal relationships, ability to love and forgive, clairsentience

Colors: Green and pink

Angel: Chamuel

The Fifth Chakra

Name: Throat chakra (Sanskrit: Vishuddha chakra)

Location: Lower part of the neck, above the collarbone, level with the thyroid, connected with the spinal cord and the extrapyramidal nervous system

Responsible for: Bronchi, windpipe, esophagus, neck, neck muscles, cervical vertebrae, jaws, ears, thyroid, larynx

Effects of hypoactivity:

At the physical level: Hypothyroidism, stiff neck, limited hearing, bronchial asthma, chronic colds

At the emotional level: Fearfulness, timidity, tendency to hold back, quietness, inconsequence, unreliability, weakness, inability to express thoughts

Effects of hyperactivity:

At the physical level: Hyperthyroidism, thyroid inflammation, larynx inflammation, esophagus cancer

At the emotional level: Haughtiness, self-righteousness, over-talkativeness, dogmatism, addiction

Effects of balanced activity: Contentment, ability to live in the moment, perfect feeling for the suitable time, ability to be a good speaker, ability to be the spiritual teacher who informs others with ease

Theme: Self-expression, communication, speaking the truth, asking for help, creativity
Colors: Light blue and greenish blue
Angel: Chamuel and Zadkiel

The Sixth Chakra

Name: Third-eye chakra (Sanskrit: Ajna chakra)
Location: Between the eyebrows and about one finger-breadth above them, with a corresponding location at the base of the skull in the area of the medulla oblongata; connected with the pituitary gland and the cerebellum.
Responsible for: Balancing the metabolism of the organs, the central nervous system, the laughing muscles, and the blood circulation of head and face
Effects of hypoactivity:
At the physical level: Simmonds' syndrome (limited physical and mental activity, no menstruation, paleness, tiredness), stunted growth, deafness
At the emotional level: Nonassertiveness, lack of discipline, hypersensitivity, extreme empathy, fear of success
Effects of hyperactivity:
At the physical level: Diabetes insipidus; gigantic growth; advanced hearing, seeing, and smelling abilities; sinus discomfort
At the emotional level: Egoism, pride, manipulation, religious dogmatism
Effects of balanced activity: Charisma, access to the source of all knowledge, telepathy, ability to travel astrally, ability to be led, independence from material things, fearlessness regarding death, connection with past lives, lack of interest in fame, luck in worldly things, mastery of self
Theme: Clairvoyance

Colors: Deep blue, indigo
Angel: Raziel

The Seventh Chakra

Name: Crown chakra (Sanskrit: Sahasrara chakra)
Location: At the crown of the head, connected to the pituitary gland
Responsible for: The healthy growth of the organs
Effects of hypoactivity:
At the physical level: Visual weakness, ocular damage, development of the wrong gender organs during puberty, brain weakness, chronic tiredness
At the emotional level: Absolute joylessness, inability to make decisions
Effects of hyperactivity:
At the physical level: Regular migraine attacks, held-back forces, head tumors, sleeping disturbances
At the emotional level: Persistent feelings of frustration
Effects of balanced activity: Openness to cosmic information, ability to overcome laws of physics, complete access to the unconscious and subconscious
Theme: Your trust in God, divine guidance, intuitive knowledge about events
Colors: Violet, white, gold
Angel: Metatron

Chakra Clearing with the Archangels

This is a very effective and intensive exercise. You must be completely ready to let go of old energies, patterns, and limiting belief systems. Don't worry about the exact wording during your meditation; the text below should help you understand the concept and serve as an inspiration for you. The archangels know your intention, and you can trust that they will do their best each time to clear and realign your chakra system, balance your emotions, remove limiting energies, help with your self-healing, and much more.

- Sit comfortably on a chair. Breathe quietly and calmly, in and out. Feel how every breath relaxes you more and more.

- Bring your consciousness to your feet, and imagine energetic roots growing from them. These roots go deep into the earth and firmly connect you with the energetic center of the earth.

- Open your feet chakras by willing it, and ask Sandalphon to clear and to cleanse these chakras.

- After that, open the chakras at your knees, and visualize stretching out your knees. Many people have energy blockages here, which is often the cause of inexplicable knee pains. You can ask Sandalphon to remove the blocking energies, and he will help you.

- Then go with your consciousness to your base chakra. Ask Sandalphon to open it wide and clear from it all harmful energies and limiting belief systems and to heal everything that is connected with it.

- Now imagine that you're inhaling deeply through your crown chakra and exhaling with strength through the base chakra. Visualize how the base chakra is cleaned.

- When you feel that the chakra is cleared and cleaned, go with your consciousness to your sacral chakra and ask Gabriel for help and support with the opening, cleaning, and purification of this chakra. Inhale through the crown chakra again, but this time, exhale through the sacral chakra.

- Now bring your consciousness to the solar plexus, the third chakra, and ask Michael, Raphael, and Uriel for help and support with the opening, cleaning, and purification of this chakra. Call Michael to your solar plexus, Raphael to your left side, and Uriel to your right side, and ask these three archangels to open, clean, and balance your whole emotional center. Inhale through the crown chakra again, and this time exhale through the solar plexus. Take enough time for this chakra, because most of what needs to be cleaned is usually located here.

- Now bring your consciousness to your heart chakra, and ask Chamuel for help and support with the opening, cleaning, purification, and healing of this chakra. Inhale through the crown chakra and exhale through the heart chakra.

- The next place you'll bring your consciousness is your throat chakra. Ask Chamuel and Zadkiel for help and support with the opening, cleaning, and purification of this chakra. The throat chakra is firmly closed for most people and thus needs special attention. To clear it and to remove the reasons for the energetic blockages might require more time. Inhale deeply through the crown chakra, and exhale through the throat chakra. Do this several times, again and again.

- Then bring your consciousness to your third eye, and ask Raziel for help and support with the opening, cleaning, and purification of this and all other head chakras (for example, the ear chakras). You might feel a pressure or even light pain at one place or another in the head area. This is normal. It merely indicates that the chakras are being worked on. Inhale over and over again through the crown chakra, exhaling through the whole head area. As you do so, sense or visualize how all head chakras are being thoroughly cleaned.

- At the end, bring your consciousness to your crown chakra and ask Metatron for help and support with the opening, clearing, and purification of this chakra. Inhale and exhale through the crown chakra again and again.

- Now ask Metatron to let pure, golden white, divine light flow from the third-eye chakra into your whole aura and body system. Feel the wonderfully powerful energy in all your cells while you visualize the cells as small, light-filled bowls which are energized, regenerated, and healthy. Feel your own God power. Feel that you are connected with the whole universe through love.

- Stay in this meditative state as long as you like, and then come back slowly into your conscious awareness.

Opening Your Energy Channels with Archangel Gabriel

You might believe that opening up your energy channels requires a special ceremony or initiation that only certain people can offer you. That is not true. Every person can open up their own energy channels. Practicing the following meditation regularly is helpful:

- Sit or lie down comfortably. Inhale deeply through the nose and exhale through the mouth. Make sure that your clothes are comfortable and that nothing can interfere with your meditation. Turn off your phone and take this time just for yourself.

- After your body is relaxed, ask Archangel Gabriel for help. Ask him to open and extend your energy channels so that they can be permeated by light in different high frequencies.

- You might perceive which colors the light has. You can intentionally visualize the colors of your chakras (red, orange, yellow, green, blue, indigo, violet/white). If you perceive primarily violet and mauve tones, this means that a transformation is taking place.

- Take enough time for this practice—about twenty minutes. Inhale over and over again, and blow out everything that has been blocking your energy channels. Ask that the opening and extension of the energy channels be done carefully and slowly.

After this meditation, energy can flow freely throughout your whole system. You will start processing and transforming old, stuck energy and replace it with new, vibrant life-force energy. It will clear your system, raise your frequency, and accelerate your healing. These processes last weeks, and as with any purification and detoxification cure, the released toxins can sometimes lead to a temporary indisposition. Memories of any former illnesses or traumatic situations might come up. Not only might the physical body show some reactions (e.g., skin rashes, flu-like symptoms), but unprocessed emotional energy can also influence how you feel (e.g., sad, depressed, angry). Be aware that this is part of your healing process and that it is very important to clear out your energy channels from harmful energies in order to stay healthy.

Taking Dead Sea salt baths (chapter 3) is a very effective way to minimize unpleasant side effects.

I recommend performing this exercise at least once a week until you can clearly feel this new level of energy and well-being.

CHAPTER 6

The Third Eye and
the Pineal Gland

Close your physical eye so you first see your picture with the spiritual eye. Then bring forth from the darkness what you saw, so that it can reflect on others from the inside out.

*—Caspar David Friedrich, Romantic
German painter (1774–1840)*

The so-called third eye plays a big role in many traditional cultures. There is a general agreement about the fact that it lays in the middle of the forehead, and that its opening leads to an increased perception of subtle energies. For our forefathers, knowledge about the third eye, spiritual visions, and other supernatural things was quite common and natural, as it still is today for indigenous people like the Native Americans and Australian natives (Aborigines).

In the course of time, people in the so-called civilized world focused mainly on material things and used their third eye less and less. As a result of not using it, the third eye was drawn deeply into the skull. The pineal gland is what remains.

pineal gland

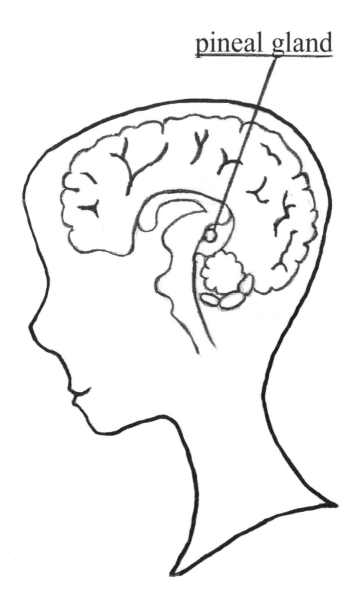

The **pineal gland** (epiphysis cerebri) is a small endocrine gland in the vertebrate brain. It produces melatonin, a hormone that affects the modulation of sleep-wake patterns and seasonal functions. It is shaped like a tiny pinecone (hence its name), and is located near the center of the brain, tucked in a groove where the two rounded thalamic bodies join. The pineal gland is reddish gray and about the size of a pea (8mm in humans). In the past, it was supposedly much larger: an inch in diameter with an average weight of 100 milligrams.

The Greeks of antiquity looked at the pineal gland as an organ, namely a kind of eye with which one could look into the nonmaterial world, as well as the seat of the soul. The anatomists of the School of Alexandria believed that the pineal gland was a valve which controlled the river of recollections. These recollections also presumably contain past incarnations.

René Descartes (1596–1650), the founder of rationalism ("I think, therefore I am."), saw a direct connection between the pineal gland and the eyes, and said, "There is a small gland in the brain in which the soul exercises its function more than in any other part of the body."

Modern research suggests that internal energy flows directly through the center of the pineal gland. Therefore, this gland is like an "eye" which is able to perceive electromagnetic fields; it can see energies of another frequency level. We are surrounded by a flood of subtle energies and information which has a constant impact on us; however, we cannot grasp it with our five senses. If we consciously lead energy through our pineal gland, we can perceive the electromagnetic fields which are surrounding us and improve our intuition. However, for most people, there is not enough energy flowing through this area of the brain because it is already blocked (by limiting belief systems, for example). The result is that what people perceive of reality is very much restricted. The activation of the pineal gland, for example, by sunlight, light meditations, Chakra clearing, and crystals, leads to an "opening of the third eye" and allows the reawakening of your spiritual and magical abilities.

Opening the Third Eye with Angel Aura Crystals

The following exercise was inspired by Doreen Virtue's "Seven steps to opening your third eye" from her book *Messages from Your Angels*.[1] I've found that additional techniques from Quantum Angel Healing enhance the effect of this exercise tremendously: Angel Breath, the Angel Healing Formula, angel aura crystals, and the help of Archangel Raziel. You will be able to receive graphic angel messages more easily and effortlessly using this exercise.

If you are fearful about seeing clairvoyantly, you should dissolve possible fears and emotional blockages with the solution formula of the angels. I recommend working with a QAH practitioner, who can guide you through this energetic transformation and help you let go of your fears.

Graphic angel messages are comparable to the pictures that you receive in dreams: you don't see them with your physical eyes, but with your inner eye. It takes a little while to get used to simultaneously seeing your client in front of you with your physical eyes while receiving an

_____
1. Virtue, 202.

angel message that you will pass on to them. The angels will only transmit energetic messages which are helpful and supportive for your client. Receiving a graphic angel message is like having a spontaneous idea or suddenly remembering an event.

There are different levels of clairvoyance, which are often described as seeing through the veils of different dimensions. Like a television set, you can intentionally turn on, off, or mute the graphic angel messages. The more relaxed you are, the easier it is to access the angelic frequencies. With a little practice, it is also possible to perceive images of all surrounding energies, for example, as colors, and to see energy beings like angels and fairies.

During the exercise to open the third eye with angel aura crystals, the client:

- sits comfortably in a chair, takes a few deep breaths, and relaxes. He knows that it is natural for everyone to receive and see inner pictures, just like in dreams, and he is ready to release all possible blockages and/or seals which might be placed on his third eye.

- does the Angel Breath and connects with his angels. He asks Archangel Raziel for help and support opening the third eye.

- relaxes and continues to breathe in and out deeply.

- releases impurities and blocking energies with his intention and breath.

- might feel warmth or tingling in his body.

- might hear angel messages and/or receive

graphic angel messages.

- might see light, colors, and angels.

During this exercise, the practitioner:

- also does the Angel Breath and connects with his angels.
- takes an angel aura crystal in his right hand and asks Archangel Raziel to send a beam of white light through it, clearing it from any absorbed energies.
- holds the angel aura crystal in his hand and puts it on his client's third-eye chakra while pointing his middle finger through the crystal toward the forehead.
- places the middle finger of the other hand at the highest point on the back of the client's head, parallel to his third-eye chakra.
- visualizes a bright laser-like beam of light coming from his right middle finger and flowing through the crystal and the third-eye chakra to the other middle finger, like a battery circuit.
- asks Archangel Raziel to intensify the beam of light with his energies and to clear all psychic debris and emotional blockages so the third eye can open. This usually takes two to three minutes.
- places his right hand, holding the crystal, above the client's right ear, sending the beam of light to the other side of the head, where the middle fin-

ger is placed above the left ear. The energy now flows through the ear chakras.

- asks Archangel Raziel to intensify the beam of light with his energies and to clear all psychic debris and emotional blockages so the ear chakras can open. This usually takes two to three minutes.

- moves both hands simultaneously to the highest part of the back of the client's head and repeats this several times in a sweeping motion. Like clearing a car's windshield of snow and ice with an ice scraper, the practitioner uses the crystal to wipe and clear the third eye, while visualizing white light permeating the back of the head. The intention is not only to clear and open the third eye, but to also hook back the third eye to the occipital lobe at the back of the head. The occipital lobe registers incoming energies and brings them into awareness through inner visions.[2]

- sets the intention to understand the meaning of the received pictures and graphic messages.

- changes hand positions again. Using his right hand, he holds the angel aura crystal over the client's third-eye chakra, then moves in a sweeping manner slowly over the third-eye chakra with the intention of removing possible seals placed over the third eye.

- asks Archangel Raziel to remove possible curses, magical apparatuses, limiting oaths, and shields of any kind that were put on the third eye by

2. Doreen Virtue explains it as follows: "Without the connection between the third eye and the occipital lobe, a person wouldn't be aware of, or understand their visions. It's like showing a movie without having the projector light on." (*Messages from Your Angels,* 204).

another person or being to prevent the clairvoyance of the client.

At the end of this exercise, the QAH practitioner and the client thank the angels for their help.

CHAPTER 7

The Tasks of the Angels

From the Bible, we know angels as bearers of messages. For example, Archangel Gabriel announced the birth of a son to Mary; angels were present at the birth of Jesus and informed the shepherds of the happy event; and angels rolled away the stone from the empty tomb on the first Easter. Additionally, angels protect and assist humans.[1] The Bible mentions different kinds of angels.[2] Nevertheless, a clear angel hierarchy is not evident in the Bible; instead, angels are distinguished by their different tasks. Seraphim, cherubim, and thrones worship God and intercede on our behalf. Dominions, virtues, and powers are leaders and protectors of all creation. Principalities, archangels, and angels watch over nations and bring messages to us from the heavenly realm.

There are some non-biblical sources that present a hierarchy within the angelic realm (e.g., the chronicles of Enoch, third century AD), which suggests that some angels might be more important than others—or are too

---

1. See, for example, Psalm 91; Daniel 6:22; Matthew (Gospel) 18:10; Luke (Gospel) 16:22; and the Acts of the Apostles 12.
2. See, among other things, 1 Samuel 4:4; Isaiah 6; Ephesians 1:21; Colossians 1:16.

far up in the hierarchy to communicate with us. Our own fears of authority and punishment, as well as the concept of "sinning," could stand in the way of healing and communication with angels. God represents the highest source of love and creation, no matter what name you might have for this source according to your religion or belief system. This love is pure and unconditional. You can trust that God always sends the right angels for your specific situation.

Every person has one or more assigned guardian angels. Many people would like to know the name of their guardian angel, but not all angels have names; however, they do have a certain function and a distinct vibration that we can become familiar with. Sometimes they take on names, making it easier for us to develop a conscious relationship with them. They also take on different forms, colors, and shapes so that we can perceive their energies with our various senses. Guardian angels offer their support and help, but would never interfere or run our lives.

We humans make our own decisions, and are responsible to discern God's ways by what the Lord has given us.3 God made us, not angels, in the image of God. Jesus makes his followers, not angels or even archangels, into God's heirs.[4] In Colossians 2:18, it says that we are not to worship angels or make them more important than God.

I also want to emphasize that there are no mean and dark angels—just like there is no dry water or cold fire. However, there are demons that can pretend to

---

3. http://www.spirithome.com/discrnmt.html

4. Are they not all ministering spirits, sent out to render service for the sake of those who will inherit salvation? —Hebrews 1:14

be angels, but unlike angels, they try to inflate your ego or divert you from Jesus or scripture, sometimes even proclaiming a new doctrine. They seize most any opportunity to rank themselves higher and instill fear in humans. Angels fight the dark and evil, but are never evil themselves; they always are beings of light and pure, unconditional love.

Most angels beam at a certain frequency, by which we can recognize them. Their energy is always affectionate, sometimes rather gentle, and sometimes very powerful. Some angels feel rather feminine, others rather masculine, but they are basically androgynous beings. They look timeless and youthful, and are always full of energy. Some wear wonderful garments and have gigantic wings; others are transparent and resemble energy clouds or balls of light.

The messages of the angels are always neutral and without judgment. They can also be amusing, comforting, or helpful. Angels never say that something must be said or done. There is no "must" in their vocabulary. They never give orders or make people's decisions—they respect the free will in all of us.

Angels are always around us and take over certain functions or tasks. They protect us, watch over us, and work behind the scenes for our highest good. They help us if we tackle new projects, search for work, have relationship issues, are in a financial predicament, need to clear our energy body, and much more. They watch over our sleep and our self-healing processes. If we are in mortal danger and our time to die has not come yet, they also intervene directly with messages like, "Pay attention to the car! Brake immediately!"

The Archangels

Archangels are usually bigger and mightier than other angels. They have a wide field of functions and tasks, which is why they are sometimes called the "managers" among the angels. The archangels often bring a whole legion of angels with them to help fulfill various tasks.

I will introduce you to the archangels whom I am in contact with below, and describe how I perceive their energy. In all my certification programs, I guide participants to get to know the archangels themselves, which is very easy to do with the help of the Angel Breath. Afterward, we compare our experiences. Each student senses something slightly different, a color, a vibration, a special message, or a gift, from the contacted archangel. Like a group of people describing the same painting in different ways, we all have our own way of perceiving energy with our different senses. The majority of workshop participants have similar angel experiences. However, some people feel the presence of Archangel Michael very strongly, while others resonate more with Archangel Raphael or Gabriel. There is no right or wrong experience—just your personal experience!

For the practice of Quantum Angel Healing, it is important that you know which angel you are connected to and who you are working with during a treatment. It's more important to be able to recognize one archangel for sure than to be uncertain about the source of energy and information you are receiving. My advice is to choose one to three archangels and get to know them really well before you expand your practice and work with other archangels or light beings.

Depending on the source of literature, you can find very different information with regard to the number of archangels. In my opinion, this happens because some angels have simply not entered our awareness or consciousness yet—just like stars and planets do not exist until they are discovered by scientists. We will discover—or become more aware of—more "new" archangels in the future.

Archangels can be in many different places at the same time, and can therefore help different people at the same time. For example, please don't think that Archangel Michael is too busy to come to you for assistance. He is always only one Angel Breath and a thought away!

If you want to call the angels for help but don't know their name or function, please don't hesitate; you can't do anything wrong. Simply do an Angel Breath, connect with God, and he will send you the angels that can support you. I've given most archangels a nickname describing their function, so it's easier for me to remember who is who in the angelic realm. The names I chose do not represent general validity; you can come up with your own names. You could call upon the angels according to the problem you want assistance with, e.g., angels of love, angels of clarity, abundance angels, travel angels, and family angels. For example, take an Angel Breath, connect to God with your heart, and say, "Dear God, please send me the angels of healing today."

Ariel

The name *Ariel* signifies "lioness of God." In the Bible, Ariel is mentioned in connection with King Solomon. This archangel is shown in pictures and artwork in connection with lions. Her energy feels rather female, clear, and certain. Ariel's aura color is pale pink, and the crystal associated with her is the rose quartz. She helps and cures animals, especially wild animals, and protects the environment. I call Ariel the Greenpeace angel, because she can clean bodies of water and protect their inhabitants, as well as help the animal species threatened by extinction. If you are involved in projects regarding environmental protection, Ariel can support you powerfully. Ariel closely cooperates with nature spirits and fairies that are known for their magical powers and can assist humans with the manifestation of their wishes.

Azrael

The name *Azrael* means "whom God helps." His energy feels comforting, quiet, and strong. His aura colors are off-white and gentle yellow gold, and the crystal related to him is the yellow calcite. This archangel has the task of supporting dying people, as well as their grieving loved ones. I call him the grief angel. He helps the dying with crossing over to the other side, relieves pain, and eases suffering. If you have lost a beloved person (or animal) and nothing makes sense to you about their death, and you are desperate and looking for answers, you can ask Azrael for help.

During times of change, many things will end and it may feel like someone or something is dying. The change could be the end of a relationship, a business, or even a neighborhood. Your ego will also have to die and sometimes let go of people and possessions. Azrael will help you during these difficult times and guide you to a better place in life. If you know anyone who is in danger of committing suicide, please ask God for help and ask Azrael for his loving support and comfort.

Chamuel

Chamuel's name means "he who sees God." His energy feels powerful and peaceful at the same time—as if nothing can really shake him. With his strong affectionate presence, he provides the feeling that nobody goes past him whom he does not want to let pass. If you connect with Chamuel through the Angel Breath, you will feel warmth and a prickle in your body immediately. His aura color changes between pale green, white, and red, and the crystal assigned to him is the green fluoride. Chamuel protects the world from frighteningly low forms of energy, and brings peace. I call him the bouncer angel because he can repulse all attacks or takeover attempts of this world or your own.

If you fear possible negative influence or disasters, you can ask Chamuel to repulse this influence and protect you. Even if you are afraid that your child, your family members, or your friends could get in bad situations, or if they're already under a negative influence, you can ask Chamuel for help. Chamuel helps create a load-bearing foundation for all your relations: in the workplace and in private life. If you have not found your life partner or your life purpose yet, you can ask Archangel Chamuel for guidance. He will help you find all you wish for, and get rid of objects and/or situations which no longer serve you.

Gabriel

The name *Gabriel* means "God is my strength." This archangel feels gentle, supporting, and rather female, but at the same time strong, as if he wants to draw your attention to something and show you the way. His aura colors are copper and yellow, and you can also perceive his energies as a pale lilac. The crystal associated with him is the citrine. In the Bible, Gabriel announced the birth of Jesus to his mother Mary, and according to the Islamic tradition, Gabriel is the archangel who dictated the Koran to the prophet Mohammed. Hence, I call Gabriel the ambassador angel.

If you have problems conceiving a child, have difficulties with pregnancy and birth, or would like to adopt a child, you should ask Gabriel for help. Also, for the "birth" of new plans and creative projects—for example, the writing of a book, the composition of a piece of music, the conception of TV or radio productions, or the creation of an art project—Gabriel stands by your side like a coach and expels fears and doubts which could cause a project delay. Gabriel ensures that creative energy flows, and that projects which help humanity and bring positive change will be successful and well received.[5]

Haniel

The name *Haniel* signifies "grace of God." The energy of this archangel feels light, patient, female, and mystic. His aura is a bluish-white color, like a beaming full moon. The healing stone assigned to him is the moonstone. Haniel supports the cycle of the woman, which is naturally connected to the phases of the moon. If you are interested in the moon, astrology, and astronomy, as well as spiritual and natural remedies, Haniel can support you with your work. If you heal with crystals or produce remedies, remedial teas, and remedial lotions, you can ask Haniel for help. If you would like to improve your spiritual abilities and strengthen your psychic gifts, e.g., clairvoyance, Haniel will guide you on how to do this.

If you have an important event coming up in your life, possibly a public appearance, an interview, or something similar, you can ask Haniel to accompany you. He

_____
5. Archangel Gabriel is also project manager of this book.

will help diminish your nervousness and surround you with harmony. I call Haniel the angel of the feminine, because he is also assigned to the planet Venus.

Jeremiel

Jeremiel's name signifies "mercy of God." His energy feels supportive and inspiring. His aura colors shimmer in a bright violet and a bright white, and the crystal related to him is the amethyst. Jeremiel helps with clairvoyance, prophetic visions, and dream interpretations. If you'd like to understand why certain events happened in your life, and if you'd like to look in the past as well as the future, Jeremiel can help you transform possible blocking emotions or limiting thought forms or programs. Jeremiel also helps you forgive yourself and others. I call Jeremiel the prophet's angel.

Jophiel

The name *Jophiel* means "beauty of God." The energy of this archangel feels uplifting, pleasant, and wonderful—as if he wants to take you in his arms and dance. His aura color is rose with gold, and the healing stone assigned to him is the rose tourmaline. His task is to cheer you up and help you think beautiful, positive thoughts. He helps dissolve negativity and chaos, as well as negative religious patterns and programs. He brings beauty into your life and pleasant experiences. If you work too much, have a lot of stress, and the world seems awful to you, call Jophiel and ask him for a transformation. I call him the good mood angel. Meditate with Jophiel, whenever you can, especially if your negative thoughts spin around in circles and you can't seem to get out of the mental merry-go-round. He can help you find creative solutions for your problems. Jophiel also serves as a protector for artists; he supports all beauty, creativity, and artistic projects.

Metatron

Metatron is an exception insofar that his name does not end with *-el.* The *-el* suffix signifies "of divine origin." Metatron has another origin: he lived as the prophet Enoch on earth. Enoch, who is described in the Bible as having "walked with God," preserved, even in his human incarnation, his God-given purity, and transformed after his death into the archangel Metatron. His energy feels strong, knowing, clear, and pure, as if he has the whole knowledge of earth inside himself. His aura colors are blue-green and rose, and the healing stone assigned to him is the tourmaline. One of his tasks consists of guarding the Akashic Chronicles, the library which contains the book of life of all life forms.

Metatron mediates between heaven and earth. He helps us understand the realms of the angels better. If you'd like to change something in your life, e.g., contracts with ex-husbands or vows which you have taken in this or in other lives, you can ask Metatron to extinguish the energetic registrations in your book of life. After this has happened, you can change your soul contract and write down your wishes and intentions so they can easily manifest in your earth life.

Metatron also helps with learning difficulties and other childhood problems. If you deal with school-children who have a hard time concentrating or are not motivated to learn, you can ask Metatron for help. Many spiritually gifted children are falsely diagnosed with attention deficit disorder (ADD) or attention deficit/hyperactivity disorder (ADHD) and then are treated with drugs. Ask Metatron for help if you deal with such children. He will help you find alternative treatments.

Michael

The name *Michael* means "he who is like God." This arch-angel has the energy of a strategist and leader, and his powerful presence is perceivable immediately—and very often connected with feeling warmth or heat. He has a golden aura with blue and some magenta; the healing stone assigned to him is the sugalite. His major task is to release the earth and her inhabitants from fear and negative energy. Archangel Michael helps all lightwork-ers, whose mission is to spread spiritual knowledge, while they work as spiritual teachers or healers (full-time or even within circles of friends and family). I call Michael the knight angel. He is often shown with a radiant blue light sword with which he can cut ethereal, energetic cords. He helps free us from negative attachments and beings, as well as all forms of fear. Archangel Michael is also the patron saint of policemen. Whenever you are in a difficult situation and feel weak and/or threatened, you can ask Michael for protection and help.

Raguel

Raguel means "friend of God." Raguel's energy feels dependable and protective. If he were to stand directly behind you, you would feel courage and trust. His aura color is pale blue, and the crystals related to him are aquamarine and the aqua aura crystal.[6]

---

6. Aqua Aura quartz crystals are created by taking natural quartz crys-tal formations and infusing them with pure gold; in a secret process which is part alchemy and part science, the two unique substances of quartz crystal and pure gold are commingled in a permanent way, resulting in the striking blue color of Aqua Aura. (The clear quartz crystal, which enters a connection with silver and platinum in a spe-cial process under pressure, gleams iridescent afterward; it is called Angel Aura.) Also see www.quantumangel.com.

He is often called the angel of justice and fairness as he helps all underprivileged and ill-treated people. Like a spiritual adviser, therapist, and lawyer, he is responsible for ensuring that everything runs in regular, harmonious ways and corresponds to the will of God. Whenever you feel unfairly treated or deceived, you can ask Archangel Raguel for help. He will help you solve conflicts, promote other people's willingness to cooperate, and clear up misunderstandings. Raguel strengthens your trust and brings peace and harmony to your everyday life. I call him the justice angel.

Raphael

The name *Raphael* means "God heals." His energy feels affectionate, gentle, and friendly, as if everything works with ease. His aura colors are emerald green and gold, and the healing stone assigned to him is the malachite. Raphael helps heal all of the illnesses from which people and animals can suffer. He supports the work of all people in healing occupations, including healers during treatments, and carries out energy healings and ethereal operations with his assistant angels. Raphael can help you decide which method of treatment to choose for a certain patient or how long a treatment should last. He consults in the production of alternative remedies and channels healing meditations through a practitioner (e.g., Quantum Angel Healer).

The archangels Raphael and Michael often work as a team to remove negative beings from people and places. If you would like to clean your home or your workplace energetically, you can ask both archangels for help. Raphael also helps open the third eye while he cures emotional wounds which could have originated from a spiritual activity in this or a former life. I call Raphael the healing angel. He is also known as the patron saint of travelers, and can provide, for example, a safe flight, problem-free transportation, and pleasant lodging for your trips. He also protects people on their inner journeys, and with their search for truth, healing, and love.

Raziel

The name *Raziel* means "secrets of God." The energy of this archangel feels subtle, mystic, and mysterious. His aura can shimmer in all colors of the rainbow, and his healing stones are the clear quartz crystal and the angel aura crystal. Raziel helps resolve spiritual and psychic blockages which often come from past lives in which healers were prosecuted, tortured, and punished because of their spiritual abilities. If you'd like to work on your spiritual abilities, Raziel can help you perceive the messages which God sends through the angels, so you can hear, see, feel, and understand divine guidance. He also helps you understand spiritual concepts and universal laws. For example, he can help you gain access to alchemy, quantum physics, and sacred geometry, while he dissolves your limiting religious belief systems. If you want to manifest your heart's desires, Raziel will guide you with his wisdom about the secrets of the universe and stand by your side. I call him the magician among the angels, because with his help, miracles happen, obstacles resolve, and you can manifest things which you thought would be impossible.

Sandalphon

The name *Sandalphon* is Greek and means "brother." Like the name Metatron, Sandalphon does not end on *-el*. As you may know from the Bible, Sandalphon was also a prophet named Elijah. You could describe the prophets Elijah and Enoch (Metatron) as brothers, who God named as immortal archangels in order to continue their sacred work on earth.

Sandalphon's energy feels very youthful and helpful. He can help you transform all of the heavy energies and emotional burdens that humans tend to carry around. His aura color is turquoise, and his healing stone is the turquoise. His major task is to carry your prayers to God so that they can be answered. Sandalphon, whose energy stretches from the heavens down to earth, brings God's answers to us—often in the form of music and inspiration. Many very well-known musicians channeled God's messages with the help of Archangel Sandalphon and translated this vibration into music. If you hear a song in your head and have difficulties understanding this form of message, you can ask Sandalphon for further clarification. You might hear the same song over and over again on the radio, on TV, in the supermarket, etc. Some of you have the mission to write your own songs and help raise the vibration on this planet through producing, singing, or playing music.

Sandalphon helps musicians with the composition of their music, especially if it is used for healing purposes. In addition, he helps cure aggressive tendencies found in some humans and animals.

Uriel

The name *Uriel* means "God is light." His energy feels protective and supportive; he wants to keep us away from harm. His aura color is pale yellow, and the healing stone assigned to him is amber. Uriel warned Noah about the menacing flood; hence, he is known as the archangel who can protect us from natural disasters like floods, hurricanes, earthquakes, and volcano eruptions. He can also help us through the aftermath of such disasters. Many people go through big life changes that feel similar to natural catastrophes, like divorce, unemployment, and illnesses. I call these events initiations: they will make you stronger on your spiritual path and help you discover who you really are. Uriel will be on your side like a coach and teacher. He can give you additional information so you are able to understand the purpose of various life lessons and initiations on earth.

Uriel will also help dissolve and transform all of the old limiting energies from situations that no longer serve you, so you can rise like phoenix from the ashes. I call Uriel the 9-1-1 angel.

Zadkiel

Zadkiel means "the righteousness of God." The energy of this archangel feels quiet, clear, and compassionate. His aura color is deep blue, and the healing stone assigned to him is lapis lazuli. The Bible describes how Zadkiel stopped Abraham from sacrificing his son Isaac. Zadkiel is also called the angel of mercy and goodwill. I use this name as well.

Zadkiel's major task is to help us forgive others and ourselves. If you blame yourself or judge other people, Zadkiel helps you transform this negative energy into compassion. Some people have a very hard time forgiving others and themselves; this is due to a subconscious program which I call the "unable to forgive program". My recommendation is to see a Quantum Angel Healing practitioner about this.

It is especially helpful to ask both the archangels Zadkiel and Michael for help with forgiveness. They are a strong team, and with their combined forces they can help you transform emotional ballast, which piles up through the inability to forgive. This negative emotional energy is a big reason why people can't heal.

Archangel Zadkiel can assist you if you have memorization issues (e.g., in school), if you have forgotten something, or believe you have lost something.

A good friend of mine loses his car keys, and especially his wallet, on a regular basis. He forgets his wallet in grocery stores, restaurants, and the post office. In the last ten years, he has lost his wallet at least a dozen times, but he has always gotten it back—though sometimes with the cash removed. However, he always gets his credit cards and driver's license back, and he's never had a problem with identity theft. One time when he was really stressed out, he forgot his wallet on the top of his car at the gas station. He got gas and simply drove away. The wallet was filled with $3,000—vacation money for him and his family. A very honest man found it at the gas station, called my friend, and gave it back. I wonder sometimes if that was Archangel Zadkiel's earthly helper.

Cherubims and Seraphims

I call cherubims and seraphims music angels because they form heavenly choirs and orchestras. They compose and play wonderful music whose energetic oscillation has a healing effect on the energy system of our body. Energy spirals which resemble our DNA form through the heavenly sounds; they penetrate every cell with harmony. With this special vibration, the angels have the possibility of changing information at the cell level and starting the healing process.

My client, Gretchen, from Germany, is a good example of how people perceive the sound and the music of Cherubims and Seraphims:

"It was in winter, 1948. My baby was only five months old. He had a bad cough and high fever. The house was cold and it was snowing again. I was sad, could not sleep, and I was worried about my child. I prayed to God and the angels for help. In the middle of the night, about three o'clock in the morning, I suddenly heard quiet music. I got up and wanted to find out where this music came from. I went to the living room where my sister slept. We had no radio and no television at this time. I went to bed again and listened to these quiet wondrous sounds for about twenty minutes. I had never heard anything like it. The next morning at breakfast, I asked my sister whether she has heard any music the night before. She had no idea what I was talking about. I did some investigation and went outside. I wanted to find out whether something unusual had taken place. To me, it seemed as if the music had been playing in front of my bedroom window. However, in the snow around the house no tracks were to be seen. Ultimately, I believed I had just imagined the music and that it was not real.

"My child slept a lot during that day, which was unusual, and he hardly wanted to eat anything. I continued to pray. The next night, I tossed and turned again because I could not sleep, and almost at the same time (four o'clock in the morning) I heard those strange sounds again.

"This time I was sure that they did not come from outside. Rather, it seemed as if the whole room was filled with them, as if the sounds wrapped my baby and me in a wonderful, warm bubble.

"I became quiet, and I felt a deep feeling of peace and confidence inside me. At that moment, I knew that these were no earthly sounds and that God had heard my prayers. I fell into a deep sleep. The next morning,

I was woken up by some noises coming from my child. However, it was not coughing. What I heard this time was a giggling, happy noise. Immediately I saw that my baby was doing so much better. The fever had broken. My heart was filled with deep gratitude for this healing. Even if I never again hear this angel's music—as I call it—I will never forget it."

CHAPTER 8

Quantum Angel Reading

Miracles are not contrary to nature but only contrary to what we know about nature.

—*St. Augustine, Bishop of Hippo (354–430)*

Quantum Angel Healing is based on the fact that matter consists of vibrating energy particles which contain certain information and sends *it out.* In a reading, the practitioner "reads" this information. It is a natural process which is supported by regular energetic cleaning, which is usually done before an energy treatment, but can be included in it, for example, when deep layers of stuck emotional energy or specific attachments need to be cleared.

During the session, a QAH practitioner has access to his clairvoyant senses. Everyone has these senses, but they are usually not trained, like unused muscles in the physical body. After an opening prayer and the Angel Breath, the practitioner receives information from the angelic realm. It is possible for the clients to ask questions about themselves, their family members, their loved ones, their friends, their animals, and souls on the other side. The angels are not limited to any dimension, time, or place. They always work with integrity and for the highest good of all. To access information, for example about a client's mother, the practitioner needs to know her first name. If it is a very common first name and more than one person in the family has the same name, it's helpful to know her age and the city where she resides. The practitioner calls in the mother's guardian angels and her higher self, always with the intention that it is for the good of all concerned. So, for example, if the client was worried about her mother, it is possible to receive information about her physical health and emotional well-being, as well as angelic advice on how to help and support her.

The code of ethics for QAH practitioners includes a respect for the privacy of a client, and a duty to never be intrusive, disrespectful, or to share their confidential information with anyone. The purpose of a QAH treatment is to enhance self-healing. The gift of Quantum Angel Healing was given to me, and it is to be shared by all QAH practitioners with love, peace, and compassion.

It is possible that clients do not want to hear the truth and advice that the angels give them during a reading. They sometimes have certain expectations and are only looking for confirmation. It is possible that they will ask for several appointments within a short period of time and consult with different readers or so-called psychics until they finally hear what they want to hear. Please do not fall for this, even if you have compassion for their situation. If they ask you for multiple sessions and suggest that they need you, it might flatter your ego or even tempt you to get more income from them; it is a trap for both of you. You do not help anyone by making a client depend on you. The temptation to accept these appointments, caused by the underlying fear of not having enough money, would only increase such behavior.

The purpose of QAH practitioners is to support other people as they discover their own healing powers, strengths, talents, and abilities. This requires becoming awake and aware; it's a process of self-realization. Self-realization means to become conscious of who you are, to realize God within, and to trust your own intuition.

Preparation

In the first chapters of this book, I explained the significance of energetic cleaning and the importance of setting an intention at the beginning of a session. Before you start with the reading, drink plenty of water, because the high energies that will pass through your body's nervous system will use this water up.

Make sure that you work in an energetically cleaned space, where you are undisturbed. It is advisable to work rested and ideally not after a big meal to increase your ability to perceive subtle energies. Many people are afraid that if they eat certain foods, like dairy products, meat, coffee, or chocolate, they will not be able to communicate with the angels. This is a belief supported by certain authors that I do not agree with. If I ask the angels to support a client in a Quantum Angel Healing session, Archangel Michael never says to me, "Oops, I cannot work with you. You had coffee in the morning and chicken for lunch. You will be punished, and I will not show up until you only eat cucumbers."

Do you understand that all forms of limiting belief systems which suggest punishment and fear do not come from God? God is the highest form of *unconditional love*. The angels are not judgmental either—only humans are.

You can drink and eat what you want according to your well-being, belief system and religion, etc. The angels will respect your choices since God gave all of us free will. However, my advice is to be mindful that everything has a certain energy and vibration. Low vibration tends to bring you down as well, especially if you have not learned how to keep your energy level as high as possible. Alcohol, legal drugs like painkillers, certain diet pills, stimulating plants, and, of course, illegal drugs, will affect your awareness and energy system. In no case should you practice Quantum Angel Healing under the influence of these substances. If you did, it's very likely that you would be unable to distinguish between an angel message and astral entities, since you would probably lose control over your senses. You would put yourself and the client in an unhealthy, unprotected, and even dangerous position.

The purer your physical body, emotional body, mental body, and chakra system is, the easier it will be for you to receive divine messages from the angels. Through a clear channel, healing energies and spiritual guidance can flow freely.

In addition, I recommend saying a heartfelt prayer prior to every reading and energy treatment. It connects you consciously with the divine source of unconditional love, it protects you against undesirable, possibly harmful, energy beings, and it reminds you that you are merely a channel (an instrument) for the angelic messages and not the origin of the information. By doing this, your ego can stay out of the way, and you can overcome emotions like pride, fear, and the need for control. You can say, for example, the Lord's Prayer or the Prayer of St. Francis:

Lord, make me an instrument of your peace.
Where there is hatred, let me sow love;
where there is injury, pardon;
where there is doubt, faith;
where there is despair, hope;
where there is darkness, light;
and where there is sadness, joy.
O, Lord
grant that I may not so much seek
to be consoled as to console;
to be understood as to understand;
to be loved as to love;
for it is in giving that we receive;
it is in pardoning that we are pardoned;
and it is in dying that we are born to eternal life.

If you have a closer connection to the female aspect of the divine energy, you can also turn to the Mother Goddess, for example, with an Ave Maria.

Use prayers which correspond to your religion and your faith, which express love and gratitude. Explain to your client that you turn to God as the source of highest love and healing energies, and that you prepare for receiving the messages from the angels.

Be cautious, however, not to push your faith and religion on your client. Respect and honor that there are many different religions and spiritual practices which might be quite different from yours.

You can always use your own words to call upon a spirit. I say something like this:

"I call upon all my angels, spiritual guides, and teachers (e.g., Jesus Christ, Archangel Michael, or Archangel Raphael). I call upon the angels of (client's name) and the higher self and angels of (name of client's family member, for example). I ask that our energy bodies are cleared and possible blocking energies or attachments are removed for good.

"I ask for this to be a sacred time and sacred space, where healing energies and unconditional love is flowing, for the highest good of all.

"I thank you with all my heart for helping my client with (the intention for the session, e.g., pain or grief).

"Thank you for your love, help and guidance. Amen."

While you are saying this prayer, you might feel and see the angels and spiritual guides entering your sacred space. You can visualize a circle of white light, a healing temple, or a pyramid of light for your sacred space. Know that you are protected at all times and know that it will be easy for you to receive divine energies and messages. You are a clear channel with pure intentions.

The Reading

After your prayer, take a few deep Angel Breaths and connect with the angels. Sense if your client is ready and open to hear the messages and guidance. You can, for example, observe their body language. If your client seems nervous and tense and has their arms and legs crossed, tell them to relax, to uncross their arms and legs, and to take a few deep breaths.

Some people who are in a crisis situation or pain might cry or shake. In this case, suggest comforting them with healing energies. Put your hands on the heart chakra and allow the love to flow through you as a channel. Within five to ten minutes, it will calm them and make them feel better. You can have your eyes open or closed to sense how your client is doing. It is very likely that you will receive messages or see pictures by simply putting your hands on your client.

You might offer your client a healing crystal of yours to hold, either to ground them or uplift them, depending on the situation. Again, trust your intuition and ask the angels for guidance. The angels might place an energetic crystal in your client's energy system or put energetic healing remedies in the aura. Some people are in so much turmoil that they have the tendency to leave their bodies—offer them some water. Check again to see if your client is ready to listen to the angels' messages. Sit across from your client. You may feel guided to hold your client's hands, but you also may not.

Ask the angels to show you with what they want to start. Maybe you will hear the names of your client's family members and sense their energy in the room. Then address their personal angels again and ask permission to ask questions, always for the highest good of all. The angels might also want to talk about a health issue, a relationship issue, or another issue. It could be that they show you symbolic pictures; for example, a candle that is burned down might symbolize that your client feels burned out. Whatever you receive from the angels, share the information with your client. You can do this and add a question: "The angels are telling (showing) me... Can you relate to this? Does it make sense to you? Do you understand this message?"

A word, a name, or a picture might not mean anything to you, but will make a lot of sense to your client. Trust the angels. They always make sense, since they see the bigger picture.

Ask your client to now focus on the subject or person that was brought up by the angels and encourage them to ask questions about it until everything is understood. Usually the angels will show you the next subject and guide you further along. Some clients want to help you, but tend to share their whole life story. Please interrupt them in this case, and help them clarify the questions which they really want to ask and have answered. Sometimes it is necessary to make it very clear that you are not a fortune-teller and that the angels do not predict the future, but remind humans how to manifest their heart's desires. Explain to these clients that they can help you the most by listening to what messages you are getting for them, and then ask the next question.

God knows everything—there is no need for explanation. The angels have full access to all information as well. You can explain that this form of communication is similar to getting information from the Internet. You just need the right web address (in this case, the first name of a person), and the angels will connect you with the energy of that person. Please remember: Everything is energy. There is no time or distance on the level of consciousness which you will be accessing through the angels.

Share the divine information you hear, see, feel, or sense. Be completely honest, but tactful. If you do not understand a message, ask your client what it means to them. You can also ask the angels for further explanation. Do not interpret anything. If you cannot make sense of a message, put it aside for now; the answer will come in a different form. It is also possible that the information will make sense to your client at a later time, sometimes months or years later. If you do want to share your opinion about a subject that comes up, please express that, but make very clear that it is not the angels speaking, but rather you expressing your personal opinion or advice.

Later on, when you have practiced communicating with angels, it will become easier, much easier, to receive messages for your client without touching them or even being in the same room; you will learn to do the same communication long distance, no matter where your client is. Be patient, and always be humble and of service. It might take a while until you become a professional at this.

I worked with clients in one-on-one sessions for more than ten years, until my life changed and I became well-known. I had my own practice in Europe, and later on in Phoenix, Arizona. I also worked with clients out of a wonderful metaphysical bookstore, A Peace of the Universe, in Scottsdale, Arizona. The owner, Judith, is famous for her hugs and for providing a safe place where people can come for guidance and support. Sometimes I refer to my time in Judith's store, where I was working as a spiritual adviser, as my "six years behind the curtain." I had no idea that God and the angels were testing me during this time. Believe me, they did in many ways. I had to face my own issues and fears, and I had to heal myself before I was ready for a much bigger divine assignment.

Since 2005, I have had a very busy international teaching schedule. I've written many best-selling books and produced CDs with Random House Europe. For practical reasons, since I am traveling so much, I specialize in working with clients over the phone. However, I recommend you get as much hands-on experience as you can with clients, before you work over the phone.

Some people use a method called psychometry. This simply means they hold a metal object in their hand during a reading, which the client uses often, like a ring, a watch, or keys. Every object they use is imprinted with the energy of the client, and it might help them access information about that person. To me, it is like using training wheels while learning how to ride a bicycle; you do not need metal objects at all to do a reading.

During countless readings over the years, I have received many interesting pictures from the angels, sometimes without a comment or message, sometimes quite unusual. It never ceases to surprise me. I remember a reading with a client named Monica. We had already talked about her health issues and their cause, when the angels suddenly showed me an interesting picture: a sticky, pretty disgusting looking, greenish substance, which reminded me of the slime I have seen kids play with at Halloween. I not only saw this green stuff, but the angels showed me, in my mind's eye, that my client was eating the green, slippery stuff with a spoon. Like I said earlier, you really have to trust your angels and honestly share their messages, even if they seem weird to you and you're afraid that you are seeing the wrong thing.

So I trusted the angels, took a deep breath to over-come my personal doubt and discomfort, and just said out loud what I saw, without knowing what it was. To my even greater surprise, the client suddenly had a big smile on her face and said, "Oh how wonderful! I know what the angels are showing you. It's my new seaweed prod-uct, which I order from California. It's really expensive, but I eat it every day. It supposedly is really good for my health, and I already feel better."

Once again, the angels had surprised me with a pic-ture which did not make sense to me at all, but it sure did to my client. Monica got the confirmation and advice that she was looking for, and continued to eat her health product.

Trust the information you are getting, even if you can-not really understand the message at first. Doubts about received information can also be dissolved by interrupting your communication for a moment, drinking a glass of water, and repeating the Angel Breath. You can then ask the angels to transform possible blocking energies, like fears, doubts, and judgments about your abilities as a reader. No clairvoyant or medium is a 100 percent clear or knows at all times exactly what spirits mean. Our brain receives information through a filter; I will explain the significance of that in the next chapter.

If you have trouble communicating with the angels, it could also be that your client's fears and energies are blocking the flow of information. I remember having two wonderful readings, but during the third, it seemed like I wouldn't be able to receive any information. I asked the client for permission to do a Quantum-Angel Healing first, before the reading, but she was not interested in getting better. Guess what her belief system was? She firmly believed that no one could help her—and she was right! Nobody could help her except for her, but it required her cooperation.

So simply do your best. The outcome of a session is not your responsibility. You are the channel for healing energies and divine guidance, but not the source!

Asking the Angels about Yourself

If you do not work with clients, but would like to receive angelic guidance for yourself, the following meditation can be very helpful for you.

- Sit or lie down in a comfortable position. Take a few deep breaths and feel your whole body relaxing—head, shoulders, neck, arms, hands, every single finger, your upper chest, your legs, your feet, your lower body, all your muscles, and your face. Your whole body will feel pleasantly warm, comfortable, and relaxed.

- Now take a deep breath and visualize a ball of light in your solar plexus. Feel now how this ball of light moves down through your body, through your legs and feet, and into the middle of the earth.

- With your next inhalation, visualize the ball of light moving up from the center of the earth, through your body and energy system, out through your crown chakra, and all the way to the divine source of unconditional love. Exhale.

- With your next inhalation, ask God and the angels to clear and realign all your chakras. Let the ball of light drop down with your breath through your whole body and visualize it moving up again. Feel how this movement transforms all stuck energies in your aura, and feel how your energy channel is cleansed. When you exhale, focus on blowing out all negative emotions, energies, and block-ages. See yourself as the beautiful, radiant, divine being you really are.

- Now see and feel the angels around you. Ask them to bring you to a sacred place where you can com-municate with them. For example, you could see a healing temple or a place in nature like a high mountain or a beach. No matter where you feel the best, always visualize yourself standing in a bright, light-filled surrounding.

- Now ask your guardian angel, Archangel Michael, Archangel Raphael, or any of your favorite angels, for their presence. Feel their energy and see them in your mind's eye. Just stay relaxed and thankful. Ask the angels for a message, for support with your healing, or simply a question.

- Spend as much time as you like with the angels. Thank them for their help and ask them to bring you back to the place where you started your meditation.

- Now feel your physical body, feel your arms and legs. Move your fingers and toes. You are now relaxed, happy, and content. You are healthy and filled with bright light, the energy of love.

If you did not receive a clear message, ask the angels to send you the information in your dreams. Also ask them for signs and messages in your daily life.

Receiving Messages from the Angels

Most people have received angel messages in their life, though many times without being aware of it. So-called paranormal abilities are actually common and quite normal. Have you ever heard the phone ring, and knew who was calling before you answered it? Or thought about a person you hadn't heard from in a long time and, out of the blue, you got an e-mail or phone call from this very person? These are signs of telepathic or supernatural abilities, which we also use to communicate with angels.

Children are highly sensitive to perceiving energies from the spirit world. Before they can express their feelings verbally, they sometimes cry and scream for reasons that adults cannot understand. It is very likely that these children see beings from the spirit world that are not angels, which scare them. In situations like these, just call upon Archangel Michael and ask him to energetically clean the room the child is in. Also, when you are leaving the house with your child, you can ask Archangel Michael for clearing and extra protection. You can visualize an additional bright light surrounding yourself and your child.

When your children speak with angels or tell you about their invisible friends, please do not doubt them, but listen, be sensitive, and take them seriously.

I remember being young and sensing spirits around me. I could feel them when my parents took me to the stores. The spirits that were passing by or went through my energy field made me feel cold throughout my entire body; I immediately got goose bumps and it made me shiver. I was not sure what caused my reaction, and neither were my parents. Instead of being understanding, they would hit me on my back and say, "Stop the nonsense. Stop shivering."

If you see your kid having a reaction to something that you can't see or explain, please consider that your child may sense more around you than you do. Your child could be one of the sensitive children known as indigo children, crystal children, or rainbow children. These children are super sensitive, highly talented, and very spiritual, and it takes great understanding to raise them. Many parents and teachers do not know how to treat them, because they are so different. Parents take their kids to a therapist and doctor in order to find a solution. Very often, these children are diagnosed with ADD (attention deficit disorder) or ADHD (attention deficit/hyperactivity disorder) and medicated to keep them quiet and numb. The medication has tremendous side effects and is harmful to these children.

Crystal children communicate telepathically, which is why they often start speaking later than other kids. Their lack of verbal communication can sometimes be mistaken for autism. Many kids from the latest generation naturally use their hands for energy healing; they treat their family members and animals. Their angels guide them as they do this.

Some people receive angel messages during their sleep in dreams or while in a trance-like state. They receive information and know about things that happened in the past or will happen in the future.[1] The received images are usually very vivid and feel real, and sometimes include symbolism. If you dream about your house or your car, understand that both symbolize your physical body. So if your car looks damaged in your dream or something is wrong with your house, it is likely an indication that you need to pay attention to your health.

If you have difficulty remembering your dreams and would like to receive messages from your angels, ask them to send their messages in a form that you can understand and remember when you wake up. You can also put a piece of paper and a pen next to your bed, so you can write down the messages immediately after you wake up, before you get up. Even if it does not make sense to you right then and there, be assured that it will later. Dreams that come up over and over again definitely indicate an important message for you that you need to pay attention to. It might be a warning, a message, or another form of guidance.

Another way to receive messages from the spirit world is through a full-trance medium, who invites a spirit being

---

1. This happens to the main character in the TV series *Medium.*

to enter their body and speak through them. Very often, the voice of the medium will change, their eyes might start flickering, and they will not remember anything that the spiritual entity has said. Whereas in half trance, the eyes of the medium are usually open and they will consciously hear, and for the most time remember, the messages. To receive messages in that way is called channeling. A human being is a conscious or unconscious channel for the spirit world.

If you want to learn how to work as a channel, I recommend that you learn from a good teacher, especially if you are interested in channeling souls that have crossed over. Channeling is a natural ability that people have, but just like riding a bicycle, it takes practice. It is safer to practice with the help of a competent instructor. Otherwise, it is possible that an inexperienced person could open up to all different kinds of spirits, and end up with unwanted attachments. This could be harmful to the medium, as well as to the client. Messages may come through, but where are they coming from? Any information is only as good as its source.

As I explained earlier, everyone can learn to fine-tune their receiver to the angels' frequency, which makes it easier to hear their messages. Communication with dead people who are earthbound spirits or ghosts trapped in the astral planes takes place on another frequency or "station." If you would like to know if your deceased family member or friend is doing okay on the other side, please contact their guardian angels first and ask them to connect you with your loved one's soul.

Spirit communication in an awake state requires some practice until you develop your spiritual muscles of clairvoyance, clairaudience, or clairsentience—which everyone can train. Sometimes you can receive angel messages as sudden thoughts, scents, tastes, or an inner knowingness, like in the following example.

Almost ten years ago, I did a reading for a client who came to see me because of her health issues. Among other things, she suffered from unexplainable skin rashes and hair loss. As always, the angels gave me messages in words and pictures, but suddenly I noticed a strange smell, which reminded me of chemicals, and sensed a funny taste of chemicals in my mouth. I knew immediately that this was a very strong angel message, because nothing had changed in my healing room and there was no other reason for this sudden smell of chemicals.

I then asked my client if she had been in touch with any chemicals lately. She denied the allegation and assured me that she lived a green lifestyle and ate organic foods and vegetables. Again, I could sense the awful smell in my nose. The client did not smell anything. Since the angels were repeating their "chemical message," I asked them to please explain what they were trying to tell me in a way that I could understand better. The angels started talking loudly and clearly into my ears and said, "Move." I shared the message and asked the client if that made sense to her.

I just want to clue you in at this point that clients might not understand, or don't want to understand, a message. Some seem to have what I call "psychic amnesia." They might have fears, doubts, or stress which can block their memory. They simply go blank and claim that they can't relate at all to your angel messages. Please do not allow that to irritate you. Just repeat what the angels tell or show you.

In this reading, the next angel message was, "Paint." The client, who was referred to me by her girlfriend, did not really believe in angels. She sat there with crossed arms. She was skeptical, fearful, and feeling very sick.

She wasn't sure if she should have spent the money on a session with me. All this attitude was like a wall of energy, a barrier, which she had put up around herself. This was why the angelic messages only came through in bits and pieces. Normally, it flows through me like a river of information.

The client was also very impatient and on painkillers, which she had taken with a couple glasses of wine prior to the reading. I saw the dark cloud in her aura field and asked her again if she had moved recently. With a bitter tone in her voice she said, "Your angels must be having a bad day today. I haven't moved in fifteen years."

I started to feel uncomfortable and swallowed down the little bit of self-doubt that I still had at that time. I asked the angels to change the subject and to show me how we could continue. (If you seem to be stuck in a reading, ask the angels and the client for the next question or subject.) So the angels started talking about my client's husband, daughter, and, finally, her son. The client was happy about the messages and suddenly seemed to be in a hurry. She explained that she needed to leave, since she had promised to help her son paint the walls in his new house.

As soon as the words came out of her mouth, the angels' messages, "move" and "paint," started making sense to her. So she told me that she was helping her son with renovating his new house, which he had bought several months ago. Her daughter-in-law was nine months pregnant, and the baby was due soon.

It turned out that all health issues my client was suffering from were caused by the highly toxic paint her son had bought at a bargain price. The young dad-to-be had saved money in the wrong place. The new baby could have died from the toxic chemical fumes that were coming from the paint. So my client went through chelation therapy and got all the toxins out of her body, and within a few weeks, she was symptom free and feeling well. She sent me a thank you note. I thanked the angels.

Is It Genuine or Just My Imagination?

A question that is frequently asked by my students is, "How do I know if it really is an angel message or just my imagination?" There are clear criteria which can help you to determine this.

To receive angelic messages, most people use one or more extended senses in addition to their normal thinking and knowing, including:

> seeing (clairvoyance)
>
> hearing (clairaudience)
>
> feeling (clairsentience)
>
> smelling
>
> tasting

The above senses work a little bit differently than what you might be used to. To feel more secure in discerning between the different types of messages, you can compare what you perceived with the following list:

Seeing (with the third eye)
words or letters written in the air

numbers written in the air

spontaneous visions

pictures from other time periods (past lives)

pictures of people, places, animals, situations which you

have not seen before

symbols

transparent, translucent colors

angels (colorful aura or lights)

energy whirls

balls of light

pictures of angels or spirit beings

shadows

silhouettes, outlines

movements you catch from the corner of your eye which tend to disappear as soon as you look straight at them

Hearing

pleasant voices in your head which other people in the room do not hear (angels do not scream or yell!)

clear, loving language

encouraging messages (no orders)

sentences that start with *we*, instead of *I*, which would indicate the ego voice of the medium

spheric sounds or music

high-pitched ringing

Feeling

pleasant tingling

increasing warmth inside of you

a breath of air

a change of air pressure

a change of air temperature

a sense that someone is observing you

a sense of a spirit presence

a sense that someone wants to say something important

a gentle angel touch

a gentle angel hug

secure and safe

protected

blissful

happy

Smelling
a pleasant scent like flowers

scents, e.g., of cigars or cologne, when you talk about another person

different smells, like chemicals, food, animals, etc., which are not related to anything which might already be in the room

Tasting
sudden inexplicable taste in your mouth which doesn't go away, even if you drink water

Knowing/Thinking
intuitive knowing (knowing information without being aware of how you could possibly know it)

sudden insights

new ideas

repetitive thoughts regarding how to help a client

reaction to prayers

answers to questions

creative impulses (for artists, musicians, etc.)

foreboding

As mentioned earlier, the angels also send their messages in the form of symbols and metaphors. For example, water symbolizes emotions.

During a recent telephone consultation, my client was in tears about her relationship. She asked me, "Why did my boyfriend end the relationship? Doesn't he have any feelings for me?"

The angels showed me an empty well, symbolizing her boyfriend. My client was looking for water, the symbol for the love she was looking for, and jumped into the well, the symbol for feeling lost and injured. The image from the angels showed that the man my client was in love with could not give her what she was so desperately looking for: love, attention, and appreciation. He had just gone through an exhausting divorce and was definitely burned out; he had nothing left inside of him to give.

The angels explained to her that this man could not give her what she needed and to leave it up to God to fill this "well"—if ever. What I understood from the angels was that she would die of thirst if she stayed, and I explained to her the seriousness of the situation. Many women wait years and hope that their significant other will change, whereas they could be really happy if they moved on to another "oasis."

Healing with the Angels

Sonia, a young doctor and first-time author, was feeling very stressed. She was emotionally blocked and was afraid of writing. Her publishing company had set a deadline for her manuscript, and she was not sure how she could possibly meet that date with all the other work she had left to do with her kids, her practice, her house, her animals, and her ill, elderly mother.

The day Sonia came to see me for a treatment was a rainy day. Her face was wet not only because of the rain, but also because of the tears running down her face. The angels helped her to relax and guided my hands to her solar plexus, where I could clearly feel a blockage. The angels downloaded pictures into my brain about one of her past lives. I asked Sonia to breathe deeply and to feel what she sensed in her solar plexus. She told me, "I see pictures. It looks like the Middle Ages, and I see myself being a monk. I know that I wrote many books." While more tears ran down her face, she continued to describe what she saw.

"I now see that the church burned all my books in a big fire. I see a mother with a little girl. The girl is ill. Although I know exactly how to help her—all the necessary information and descriptions of healing remedies are in my books—I just stand there and say nothing, knowing that the little girl will die without the herbal remedies."

My client Sonia felt guilty and cried more. The angels asked her to forgive herself, and transformed all of her blocking emotional energy and moved it out of her cellular memory and energy field. This QAH treatment helped dissolve the writer's block caused by her stored emotional energy. From then on, it was easy for her to bring forth her valuable knowledge about herbal remedies in her first book.

Healing Cancer with the Power of the Angels

Barbara from Massachusetts had terminal cancer. Both of her breasts had been removed and her chemotherapy was not successful. Her ex-husband came to the hospital every day and was finally able to express his feelings for her: He was full of love and gratitude for his ex-wife, who had supported him all the way through college so he could become an architect. His work took him around the globe, and Barbara raised their little daughter more or less by herself.

Barbara never gave up and believed that she could be healed. She prayed to God and talked to the angels every day, asking for help.

One night, she became aware that somebody had come into her room, even though she had not called for a nurse. She was only half awake when she saw a pink angel lean over her and whisper, "Breathe with me in this rhythm. I will remove your tumors and you will be healed."

Barbara thought she was dreaming, but followed the angel's instructions. She breathed in and out deeply just like she was shown.

And again she heard the angel's voice. "Please come with me and see yourself walking in a beautiful meadow. You can see many white flowers and the gentle, beautiful colors, and hear the singing of the birds as they fill your heart with joy.

"Then you come to a valley. It is the valley of death. There you put down your clothes and your physical body. You then go up the mountain and feel how wonderful it feels to be free of your burden and pain. All heaviness is gone and you are ready to take on a healthy body. You breathe deeply in and out and feel that purity, clarity. Health floods your consciousness. It's like you notice a cloud of energy—a cloud of little golden particles which consists of pure consciousness—which you now slowly breathe in. The vibration is very high and at first you have to adjust to it. The golden particles function like little magnets and attract other cosmic substances to form a young, healthy body. The water element takes a big part in building this new body. The water is clean and comes from a pure source. The gentle vibration in all cells contains the information: 'I am a divine being and create for myself a healthy body for this incarnation.'"

After the journey with the pink angel, Barbara felt a little weak at first. Something had happened to her that she could not explain.

Her "dream" left a beautiful flower scent in her room. When she moved her hands and fingers, she noticed that her wedding band fit much looser, and that the scars from her operation did not hurt her anymore. It felt as if she could get up without any headache or dizziness. She was already walking down the hallway before she realized that her whole body had changed and that she looked different.

That morning, nothing was like it was before. Barbara's husband was called and told to come to the hospital immediately. The nurse told him on the phone, "A miracle has happened. You need to come right now." At first he thought it was a bad joke, but when he saw his wife standing at the window smiling at him youthfully, he also believed that a true miracle had happened.

In many cases, tumors lead to the death of a cancer patient. The disappearance of a cancerous tumor is always looked at as a miracle. And yet, these miracles happen over and over again. True stories like this are proof that energy, breath, intention, prayer, love, and gratitude, as well as God's grace and the support of the angels, can change a person's health and life.

CHAPTER 9

The Power of Subconscious Programs

Common sense is the collection of prejudices acquired by age eighteen.

—*Albert Einstein (1879–1955), German-born American physicist*

Many people who want answers from the angels ask questions like: Why am I constantly ill? Why do I always fall for the same kind of men? Why do I suffer from a chronic shortage of money? These people are searching for the reasons for their suffering, their illnesses, their pains, and their difficult life situations. They want to learn how they can solve these problems and cure themselves from illnesses.

In the previous eight chapters, I've written about the foundational techniques of energy healing, including energetic clearing and the importance of raising your frequency, as well as the archangels and their different tasks. This chapter will guide you to the essence of Quantum Angel Healing and uncover emotions, thoughts, and programs. If this book was like an ordinary cookbook, all you would know by now was different cooking techniques and new recipes. However, if you use the same old pots and pans, and fill them with the same ingredients, it is very likely that you will cook the same old soup over and over again. What does it mean in our context?

You probably know people who are always sick or seem to have one illness after the other. They spend a lot of time at the doctor's office. They talk about their illnesses all day long, and by doing that, they give more and more energy to this subject—like pouring fuel onto a burning fire. They wonder why no one seems to be able to help them and why the reason for their illnesses can never be found. Then, there are the "lucky ones," who seem to never have any health issues. Why not?

Other people always have money issues. They have a hard time paying their rent and bills every month. Usually their debts increase more and more, they lose one job after the other, and they look for someone or something they can blame for their misery: stupid coworkers, an unreasonable or mean boss, the bad economy, etc. But no matter how difficult the global economic situation may be, there are always people who earn—or just have—lots of money. What Is the Difference?

To answer the above questions and to find out what each of us can do to change our problems for good, let us investigate the true reason for various miseries.

In one of my QAH sessions with a client, the angels explained the reason for the client's reoccurring problems with an example from nature. Imagine mowing the lawn, including the yellow dandelions. It is not enough to just cut off their yellow heads with the lawn mower and hope they are gone forever. This would equal the common practice in medicine of just treating a symptom (e.g., with painkillers) or removing bad tissue from a patient's body and hoping the problem is solved for good. If you don't take out the dandelion roots, they will continue to spread all their seeds, and create new dandelions that grow everywhere. The same is true for people's problems. First, you have to find the true cause for a problem, and then you have to remove the roots. In Quantum Angel Healing, the root of a problem or illness is identified with the help of the angels and removed by energetic transformation.

Self-Knowledge Is the First Step Toward Recovery

The following research of Dr. Bruce Lipton, Dr. Deepak Chopra, and Dr. Candace Pert outlines the important scientific knowledge Quantum Angel Healing is based on. Several examples of QAH treatments demonstrate how this knowledge can be applied and have powerful, life-changing results.

Dr. Bruce Lipton, a cell biologist, made it very clear through his work that we are not the victims of bad genes which we have no control over. His work is based on the revolutionary scientific discoveries of epigenetics. This means that it is not genes which cause an illness, although that was the common belief system for many decades. Doctors used to explain a health problem simply by saying that it was inherited and that there was nothing they could do about it. The truth is, over 90 percent of all illnesses are caused by so-called epigenetic factors.[2]

Epigenetics prove that—above genes—environmental signals activate cell membranes' switches, which send secondary signals to the cell nucleus. Inside the cell nucleus, these signals then select gene blueprints and

2. *Epi* in Greek means "over" or "above."

control the manufacturing of specific proteins. So no genes turn themselves on or off; it is our environment that triggers a chemical reaction within our bodies. Genes are comparable to the blueprint of a house drawn by an architect; they are simply a plan. They are not the contractors and handymen who actually construct the house.[3]

So what can we do to build the house, body, or life that we really want? Who influences the environmental signals that control the building blocks of our bodies? How can angels give us the answers and help us?

"Self-knowledge is the first step toward recovery" is what I heard over and over again during my childhood, but it wasn't until many years later that I understood the meaning of the phrase. At first, I was very upset when I learned that *I* created everything that was going on in my life. So have you, and no one else is to blame!

After a severe, life-threatening illness, I wanted to blame everybody around me, but then I started to look for the reason why it had happened to me. It took years of self-discovery, studying natural medicine, and a lot of spiritual growth until I found out that all problems and illnesses are created through our belief systems and programs. They are mirrored in our environment and signaled back to us. Behind them is the powerful energy of our subconscious emotions, which, when released, trigger the signals influencing our cell activities. One of the biggest emotional land mines within our system is fear.

I want to focus first on the origin and meaning of buried emotions, which are the energetic building

---

3. Bruce Lipton and Steve Bhaerman, *Spontaneous Evolution: Our Positive Future (and a Way to Get There from Here)*, Carlsbad, CA: Hay House, 2009.

blocks of our belief systems, thought forms, and subconscious programs. I want to remind you that all emotions are simply energy which cannot be destroyed, but merely transformed. You probably have more questions about this, which I would like to answer.

Is There Really a Difference Between Feelings and Emotions?

There are definitions according to which feelings are positive (for example, love, joy, trust, courage, harmony, patience, and confidence) and emotions are negative (for example, anger, fear, jealousy, revenge, grief, annoyance, and frustration).

I do not agree with those definitions, because they contain a judgment which is not consistent. According to which criteria should one judge whether a feeling is positive or negative? Some people look at the emotion of grief as something negative. For others, the same emotion is helpful and important, and therefore positive.

I look at feelings or emotions without judging them. To me, they are energies in motion (*e-motion = energy in motion*). They can set a lot of things in motion, but they can also block us. In this book, I primarily use the word *emotion,* which also encompasses feelings for me.

Energies move in waves and have certain frequencies. The frequency of the waves and the size of the area between the single waves give information about their intensity. If you look at sound waves graphically, it becomes clear that the higher the tone or frequency, the narrower the waves are. The respective human value system decides whether this energy is positive or negative.

Where Do Emotions Come From?

Many of our emotions and programs originate from before our birth. We have brought them into this life. In clinical studies, therapists have proved that under hypnosis, their clients have access to stored information and emotions from former lives. In so-called past life regressions, clients gave detailed information about their lives and how they died. In Eastern religious traditions, e.g., Tibetan Buddhism, there is no doubt about the reality of reincarnation. It is simply a matter of awareness or ignorance. The spiritual leader of the Tibetans, the current and fourteenth Dalai Lama, is recognized as the reincarnation of the eighth Dalai Lama.

Other therapists and scientists in the Western world have done research on the prenatal phase which shows clear evidence that babies are emotionally influenced before birth. Why is it that adults usually have no conscious recollection of their prenatal time? In his book *The Secret Life of the Unborn Child*, Thomas Verny presents the origin of consciousness of a human being. He explains that during labor, the mother's body releases the hormone oxytocin, which activates the contractions. This hormone is also responsible for erasing the present memories of the baby, including that of former lives. During birth, the baby is flooded with this hormone.

Another hormone secreted by the mother's pituitary gland during labor is adrenocorticotropic hormone (ACTH), which regulates the production of stress hormones, especially during times of biological stress. The stress hormones (corticosteroids and cortisol) enhance the baby's memory. Every time the mother experiences fear or stress, large amounts of stress hormones are released to the bloodstream of the baby. As a result, the subconsciousness of the child can retain information very well, which has a large impact later on.

My client Susan came to me with her nine-year-old son Sebastian. She was desperate and looking for help through Quantum Angel Healing. She was anxious about her son, who was not behaving like others in his age group. Every time she wanted to leave a room, he would start crying and screaming, "Please don't leave me." The daily good-bye routine before school was dramatic and never without tears for the boy. It was torture for him. He was also extremely fearful of water and fire.

During Sebastian's energy treatment, the angels showed me pictures from one of his former lives. As a helpless child, he had to watch how his parents burned in their farmhouse. He could not extinguish the fire; the flames were too high. This trauma was deeply stored in Sebastian's cells and affected his behavior in this life. Every time he had to say good-bye to his mom, an extreme fear of loss came up for the little boy, as if he would never see her again.

With the help of the angels, the cause for Sebastian's unusual behavior was found and the emotional energy was transformed. His behavior is fine now, and he is happy and free of the old fears.

My client Iris, twenty-eight, was born two months too early. She came to my practice because she searched counsel with regard to her professional life. It turned out, that she had dropped out of high school and all the other educational programs that she tried out after that. She was always fearful about exams and could not finish her papers. Her first divorce happened when she was twenty-seven.

Iris was frustrated and had such a hard time finishing anything in her life. She couldn't even visualize finishing anything; it all appeared to her like a dark hole. The subconscious fear and picture of the "dark hole" was a stored memory originating from her premature childbirth; it became a program which repeated its pattern over and over again in her life. Everything in her life ended prematurely, and it influenced her whole life. With the help of energy work and angel's healing, these dammed-up negative emotions were released and transformed. She learned to visualize, and for the first time in her life, she saw light at the end of the black tunnel.

My friend Melanie shared with me another example of accessible memories deriving from the time of birth. During the birth of her long-desired child Morton, there were some complications. He needed an operation immediately after his birth, and he spent the first weeks of his life in the intensive care unit of the maternity clinic.

When Morton was two and a half years old, Melanie showed him a photo album with the pictures she had taken during the previous years. When he saw the pictures of himself in an incubator in the intensive care unit after his surgery, he started to cry and shouted, "Baby wants his mummy." Morton expressed the emotions he'd had in his first days of his life. They had been dammed up since then, because he had not been able to express them as a baby. Only now, Melanie could comfort him, take him in her arms, and give him all the love he needed.

Where Are Emotions Stored?

Every emotion and every thought sends a message to every cell of our body. These messages have more or less intense consequences for us, and it doesn't matter whether we consciously remember this or not. In any case, the sent emotions are registered in the DNA of our cells and their intensity dictates the amount and strength of the equivalent energy that is stored.

In his book *Quantum Healing,* Dr. Deepak Chopra explains the function of DNA and RNA. RNA is responsible for the production of more than two million different proteins which form and repair the body.

RNA is the active consciousness; DNA is the silent intelligence. Through the cooperation of DNA and RNA, cells know how, and in which way, they must function, not only during the growth phase of a person, but also during crises like traumas, illnesses, accidents, and emotional stress. DNA contains the blueprint, and has, so to speak, the architect's plan in its hand, while RNA explains the construction work.

In addition, there is the body-mind connection with DNA. We communicate regularly with the DNA in all our cells. If the brain didn't send out neuropeptides as ambassadors, neither a thought nor an emotion would originate. All life originates from the DNA which is in every single cell, and every single cell is influenced by every thought and every emotion.

In her book *Molecules of Emotions,* Dr. Candace Pert debates whether emotions originate first in the head or in the body, and where they are stored.

While scientists like Paul McLean believe that the seat of emotions is in the so-called limbic system of the brain, the research results of Dr. Pert, a neuroscientist, have proven that emotions are stored all over the body, distributed in so-called nodal points. Pert explains that there is a psychosomatic network in the body and that it depends on the receptors of the neuropeptides whether a thought or an emotion becomes conscious or is stored as an undigested pattern at a deeper level in the body.[4] Within this network, emotions and body sensations are interwoven with each other; one influences the other. The easiest way to access the stored subconscious emotions in the cells is through therapeutic touch of the body in connection with high energy (one element of QAH). Unfortunately, conversations, affirmations, or both, do not help every client.

What Is the Brain's Filter System?

Every second, our senses take in millions of pieces of information, which are processed and stored depending on their different priority. All sensorial information goes through a filtering process and is passed on via numerous synaptic connections, until it finally reaches our consciousness. Our religious belief systems and present experiences influence our perception of it.

The successful movie *What the #$*! Do We Know!?*, which is about the connection of quantum physics and spirituality, demonstrates clearly that we only perceive what we believe exists. The movie shows a group of natives standing on a beach and looking at the sea. The shaman of the tribe excitedly points over and over again at the movement of the water; however, the people on the beach are unable to recognize the cause for the waves. Only the shaman, who was used to opening his consciousness for more than just everyday things, could perceive a big sailing ship on the horizon that was causing waves. The other tribesmen did not recognize the ship because it had not existed in their world up until that point.

---

4. Pert, Candace, Molecules of Emotions, Simon & Schuster, 1999.

If there is no concept to relate to, information simply cannot be processed. Just like if you hear a language that you don't speak, you will hear the sound, but you will not understand a word. This is also the reason why many people cannot see angels. A filter is inserted in their brain which prevents their deliberate perception of the visual information because it possibly believes "Angels do not exist or angels are invisible."

During the first day of the certification program in Quantum Angel Healing, I explain the function of this filter, while showing pictures like the one on the next page. I ask, "What do you see in this picture?"

The result of this experiment is always similar. Almost all participants immediately recognize the birds, clouds, and the sky. After a little consideration, many have an "aha" moment and shout, "This is an angel!" We all have lots of fun with one another afterward, for it takes everyone a different amount of time until they can happily say, "I have it! Now I also see an angel."

However, in every workshop, there also are some participants who have difficulty perceiving the angel after their brain has decided that the picture shows birds. Their brain's filter prevents an enlarged perception of what is. There is no objective reality. This is also true for the perception of angels. If people have a fear of seeing angels, the filter of their brain will accordingly not allow them to see an angel. What a person considers as real is always filtered by past emotions, experiences. and religious beliefs.

The typical fears which block the perception filter for angels are:

- Fear of seeing something awful
- Fear of being ridiculed
- Fear of not being able to turn off their perception
- Fear of being punished by God
- Fear of being able to predict events (especially of frightening things)
- Fear of having to be responsible
- Fear of failure

These fears are mostly hidden, and people often try to conquer them with another belief system: "You must try harder and more often to compensate." However, the perception of angels cannot be forced. The more one tries and forces himself, the greater the blockage becomes. People who want to communicate with angels need help resolving their fears and limiting religious patterns, and help healing their psychic blockages. Once this occurs, their heart chakra and third eye can open, and the limiting brain filters will disappear.

How Do Emotions Influence Our Lives?

We all carry around stored emotions and programs, which make life needlessly difficult for us. These stored emotions form our belief systems and patterns which determine our thoughts. The thoughts are like seeds which we plant in the fertile ground (emotion), which has been prepared since our conception, and they grow when we feel intense emotions (for example, fear). If the energy of these emotions meets thought, they generate a vibration which has a magnetic effect again, and always draws exactly to us what we think. In this manner, we create our reality. If our reality looks different than what we wish it to be, this is due to the fact that our emotions and our thoughts do not agree. If we direct our thoughts, for example, upon something that we would like to have, but subconsciously the emotion rules that we are not worthy of the desired object, we will not get it. Do you know the expression "He's out of his mind"? It expresses that emotions propel us, but contrary thoughts cause a conflict.

Quite often, we act in spite of good intentions or "against better judgment," and end up with guilt. Have you ever asked yourself why positive affirmations function for some people, and for others, not at all? For the people who do not achieve desired results in spite of positive affirmations, emotions and thoughts run in different directions. Where the affirmations are successful, emotions and thoughts agree. To deliberately manifest your wishes (for example, for the curing of illnesses), emotions and thoughts must agree. This was also explained in connection with the meaning of intention (see chapter 1).

If you are constantly disappointed in relationships, if everything seems to go wrong, or if you never achieve the desired results and are always frustrated, your thoughts and emotions run with certainty in different directions. The rule of thumb, "always think positively," is certainly not the universal remedy to gain control of the world of thought.

Sometimes it can be of importance to express long-suppressed pain, annoyance, and other feelings, even through screaming and hitting (ideally not a living being; I suggest a pillow), so that they do not manifest themselves as illnesses, escalate, or get out of control.

We all know about the red buttons that will cause us to explode, especially if they are pressed by people close to us (spouse, children, parents, etc.), even without any evident emotional reason. Behind such explosions are always concealed pain and hidden wounds that are not healed.

Mandy, thirty-two, longed for an understanding partner for many years; however, it seemed as if men avoided her as much as they could. Desperately, she looked for the causes and seriously thought that something was wrong with her. In fact, Mandy scratched herself sore regularly. The scabby and scarred skin on her arms did make her less attractive to most men; however, this was not the reason why she couldn't engage in close relationships with men. During the energy treatment with the angels, it turned out that Mandy had been sexually abused by her father at the age of three. She had not had any recollection of this experience; however, the long-suppressed memories and emotions were released in the form of internal pictures which she had stored inside of her subconsciousness.

At first she felt nothing but a paralyzing helplessness because she recognized that she had not been able to defend herself as a child. However, an unbelievable anger overcame her shortly after that. The angels encouraged her to let out this suppressed energy. They asked me to hand Mandy a pillow with which she could let out her anger. The pillow was a surrogate for her father. She pounded on the pillow while screaming loudly, "I hate you. I hate you. How dare you touch me."

She cried as she continuously beat up the pillow over and over again, harder and harder, until she was able to let go. Mandy continued to cry like a hurt little girl and lay down and curled up in the fetal position. I put a blanket over her and she cried for another ten minutes until all the energy was released and she felt empty, but also calm and free. Her suppressed emotions were released with the force of a volcanic eruption.

Experienced Quantum Angel Healing practitioners know how to handle a situation like this, and they always follow the angel's guidance.

The angels continued the treatment with Mandy and removed all the remaining energy and emotions connected to her childhood experience and other negative experiences with men. Then they guided Mandy through a healing meditation and applied the angelic solution formula, with whose help she could forgive her father and herself.

Within ten days, all her abrasions healed, and a little later, she let me know about her new nice boyfriend, whom she was starting to get to know, little by little. He was also abused as a child, and has a lot of understanding and love for Mandy.

How Can We Change Our Thoughts and Emotions?

If we are unhappy about what we create day in and day out, on behalf of our unaware and undesirable emotions, we should transform these emotions and their energetic impact. During the treatment with the angels, we can go back to the origin of the emotions and change their vibration. (How it works is explained in chapter 14 on pages 191 ff..) This process changes the information stored in the subconsciousness, and with it, unwanted emotions and programs.

Of course, we can also change our thoughts by affirmations; however, the thoughts will appear again if we do not transform the emotions and their energetic origin. In other words, if we do not extract the dandelion with the root, it will grow over and over again.

Because of difficult and traumatizing experiences, many people have obstructed access to their emotions. For them, it sometimes seems better to feel nothing than to feel pain. Also, social restrictions have caused men to separate themselves from their emotions; they are often called "softies" or "crybabies" if they express their feelings. Many men were programmed during infancy, by mockery and punishment, to suppress their emotions. These buried or consciously suppressed emotions cannot be turned off or simply swept under the carpet. Their energy is stored in the body and energy field of the person concerned. The emotions leave not by themselves, but, on the contrary, extend more and more. It requires more and more strength to keep them in secrecy—strength which the body loses. The body becomes weaker and weaker and, in the end, even gets ill. For example, a situation in the workplace feels stressful. Stress means that we suppress our emotions and do not say or act out what we are thinking. As everyone knows, the main cause of myocardial infarctions is stress.

Emotions are energy which does not disappear by itself; however, this energy can be transformed. It is possible to change emotions and the programs linked with them, and to therefore cure the cause of illnesses and solve problems permanently.

The first step to transforming emotions is to be ready and to realize them, as well as admit them, without assessment or conviction (see also healing and deleting of the judge program, page 174). Only then can you realize what you would like to feel instead.

I explain this to my clients with the example of a flower vase. Before new water and new flowers can be placed in a vase, the old flower water must be poured out. In his book *Perfect Health*, Dr. Deepak Chopra writes that in the DNA of every cell, the memory of the perfect blueprint is stored; it is merely covered by the energy of different programs which stop the cells from functioning perfectly. [5]

Checklist of Unwanted and Unresolved Emotions

Many people wish nothing more than to be loved, healthy, and free; however, they often carry around undesirable and unreleased emotions which hinder them from

---

5. Deepak Chopra, *Perfect Health*, (New York: Three Rivers Press, 1990).

achieving exactly that. This emotional luggage they travel with can have extremely negative consequences for their future journey, including tension; a lack of spontaneity, creativity, and joy; and even physical illnesses.

Please check which of the emotions below you or your clients carry around. After you have identified your "luggage," you can choose how you would like to feel instead, and put this in a healing solution formula, like one of the following:

> I feel (accepted, protected, cured, beloved, understood).
>
> I am (grateful, healthy, happy, successful, calm, fully illuminated, certain).
>
> I decide to be (courageous, fit, financially independent, free, productive, mobile, strong).

Always formulate your solution formula positively, and remember: You create your own life!

Emotions:

abandoned

accused

afraid

agitated

aimless

alarmed

alone

angry

annoyed

anxious

apprehensive

ashamed

attacked

awful

bad

banished

beaten down

belittled

betrayed

bewildered

bitter

blocked

bored

boxed in

brutalized

burdened

burned-out

careless

chaotic

cheated

childish

clingy

closed off

clumsy

compromised

compulsive

conflicted

controlled

cranky

crazy

criticized

crushed

cursed

deceived

defeated

degraded

demoralized

denied

dependent

deprived

deserted

despair

destroyed

devalued

different

dirty

disappointed

disapproved

discontent

discouraged

disgraced

disgusted

dishonest

disorganized

disrespected

dissatisfied

disturbed

dominated

drained

embarrassed

empty

enslaved

envious

excluded

exhausted

exploited

exposed

failure (like a)

fatigued

fearful

filthy

foolish

forgotten

fragmented

frantic

frightened

frigid

frustrated

furious

grieving

grouchy

guilty

gutless

harassed

hate/ful

heartbroken

helpless

homeless

homesick

hopeless

horrible

horrified

humiliated

hurt

hysterical

ignored

imbalanced

immature

immobilized

impatient

imprisoned

inadequate

incapable

incompetent

incomplete

indecisive

ineffective

inferior

insane

insignificant

insulted

intimidated

irritated

jealous

joyless

lacking (of)

left out

less than

let down

limited

lonely

longing

loser (like a)

lost

luckless

mad

manipulated

melancholy

miserable

mistreated

misunderstood

misused

naive

neglected

nervous

not good enough

numb

offended

oppressed

outcast (like a)

out of control

overwhelmed

overworked

oversensitive

paranoid

persecuted

poor

powerless

pressured

punished

pushed

quitter (like a)

rejected

restless

restrained

ridiculed

rotten

ruined

rushed

sabotaged

scattered

scorned

self-conscious

self-destructive

self-doubting

self-loathing

separated

shameful

shocked

shunned

speechless

stressed

struggling

stuck

stupid

suffocated

suppressed

tense

terrible

terrified

threatened

tired

tormented

trapped

troubled

ugly

unaccepted

unappreciated

uncomfortable

undesirable

unfulfilled

unhappy

unlovable

unnoticed

unpleasant

unproductive

unprotected

unsatisfied

unsuccessful

unsupported

unwanted

unworthy

upset

used

useless

victimized

violated

void

vulnerable

weak

worried

worthless

wounded

CHAPTER 10

The Victim Program

The victim program is widespread especially among women, and is also called the "good girl program." As children, the women who were subconsciously programmed by their environment suppressed their needs. As adults, they sacrifice themselves—for their children, husband, and job. They are exhausted and frustrated; they give everything and get back nothing. Still, they try to give more, because they hope that the love which they give and for which they look, will someday flow back to them.

Often one can recognize this program by someone's posture, but also by other physical symptoms. These people tend to have migraines, back and shoulder problems, and often walk bent forward. They carry the emotional load of their family, and sometimes even of their whole work environment: company, healing practice, hospital, church, or charity organization. Does that sound familiar to you?

Martha, sixty-nine, is the archetype of the victim program—she was never employed, yet worked around the clock. Women like her work unpaid as housewives in the family or in an honorary capacity, e.g., in the community or for the church, without really finding personal fulfillment in their work.

Martha was raised on a farm. From an early age, she knew nothing but work. Her mother had died when she was twelve years old. She had been a substitute mother for her four younger brothers, who were nine, seven, five, and three years old at the time of their mother's death.

For a few hours in the early morning she went to school, and then spent the rest of the day working in the fields, feeding the animals, cooking for her brothers, cleaning, and washing tons of laundry. In the evening, she was exhausted yet went to bed late, since her father felt lonely and wanted her company.

Free time was a foreign concept to Martha. She always had to put her own needs last. Also, in her later life, it was almost impossible for her to be cheerful, to enjoy something, or to express her own wishes. She developed the belief system "life is work," and an emotional addiction to being needed. She did not choose her later husband because of love. Rather, she obeyed her father, who wanted his daughter to marry a housepainter. The housepainter had asked her father for his daughter's hand in marriage. At the same time, he had offered to paint her father's house for a very special price. What a great deal!

After her brothers grew up, Martha's son was her whole purpose in life. Martha felt the happiest when she could cater to him. She made him homemade cake and did his laundry, even after he had moved to his own apartment at age thirty-nine—under major protest from his mother. Even after he had moved out, Martha called her unmarried son several times a week to remind him to bring her his dirty laundry on Saturday morning, and, of course, to remind him to show up on Sunday at noon for the family lunch. Later, on Sunday afternoon, he could take his freshly ironed laundry back to his apartment.

Martha controlled her son's life and sacrificed herself for others, until her undigested emotions caused colon cancer. After several operations and lots of suffering, her unfulfilled life came to an end.

To sacrifice oneself in everyday life or in a badly paid job is a typical sign of the victim program; however, the so-called victims are not really unselfish. Mothers, for example, often cling to their children in whom they have invested so much work and time. With this behavior, however, they don't generate self-confident, free people, but rather new victims who have difficulties realizing their own needs, because they unconsciously try to always satisfy their mother (or other person in a position of authority) or make someone else happy.

On account of the characteristic feature of the victim program (victims do not allow themselves to have "selfish" joy), it is not possible to make victims happy. For example, no matter how hard a child tries to do something wonderful and make Mama happy, they will never be successful. This becomes the belief system of the next generation. It is a tragic cycle. Without major healing and transformation, the victim program is passed on from generation to generation.

Maybe you ask yourself what is wrong with wanting to help family members and other people. Nothing at all. It is not about whether it is right or wrong. You generally do not need to change anything, but maybe you can think about how you can improve things in your life and have fun, love, time, health, or money, and also still have all the other things that you wish for your personal happiness.

My teacher Zohar explained to me many years ago that it is important to be able to give and receive equally. How would the world look if we only were able to give?

And how would it be if everyone only took? We all contribute to the balance in this world while we bring ourselves into balance.

People whose lives are determined by the victim program suffer from a lack of energy, which also expresses itself as a lack of time and a shortage of money. In my workshops, we practice the following self-analysis:

- Determine what percentage of the daily energy which you have at your disposal flows in different directions. Take a sheet of paper and draw yourself in the middle of a circle on the sheet. Then, around you, arrange other circles which represent partners, children, occupation, household and honorary (unpaid) activities, family members, friends, etc.

- Mark what percentage of your energy flows away from you and how much comes back. Add the percentages.

How much energy do you have at your disposal at the end of the day? Is it 5, 10, 20 percent or even more? Or are you in the deficit, at less than 1 percent? I've seen the results of many people and found out that most of them are energetically bankrupt. They give substantially more than they get back; they feel empty, stressed, and become ill.

Would you like to change something for yourself in this regard? Then create a new list with ten points, representing the "circles" in your environment (spouse, children, job, etc). You are number one on the list. Imagine that you are healthy and ideally have a hundred percent energy. The number two on the list is the second most important person or activity in your life, number three is the third, and so on. Remember, you are most important to yourself. Now write how much of your energy you are willing to give to numbers two through ten. Be careful: you can't spend more energy than you have on others. At least 51–100 percent of your energy should be available to you. Also take into consideration that some people and tasks in your life send energy back to you. Be honest! Now you have a good picture of your energetic situation. Please decide whether you can afford to give your energy, your time, and your money.

In order to no longer be a victim, first make sure that everything goes well for you; get enough sleep and eat well so that you can charge your own batteries. This can happen in different ways. For example, you can meditate, walk, practice yoga, or rest while you follow your passion.

To all who now might think, "This won't work for me. I have no time," let me share a secret with you that I learned at a conference in Los Angeles from the best-selling author and multimillionaire, Jack Canfield: Jack divides his week into three focus days, two "whatever" days, and one holiday day. During the focus days, he attends meetings and appointments. He gets 90 percent of his professional tasks done, because he knows that the next day is a holiday day. During these days, he concentrates on nothing else, and also doesn't postpone anything to the next day or later.

Certainly you have also already had the experience that you can accomplish things with unbelievable intensity before you go on vacation. Is it not interesting that we can work off long lists and create a lot before it is time to go have fun? If you work for three weekdays with this intensity, the efficiency of your work increases about a total of 65 percent.

During the "whatever" days, there is time for shopping, the tennis club, friends, the hairdresser, continuing education, etc., as well as time to accomplish things like the remaining 10 percent of your work.

During his vacation day, Jack keeps himself really free for one day. This is a day without phone calls, e-mails, or other professional obligations. He is simply not accessible for twenty-four hours and does only what is great fun to him, including having sex. During such days it is also possible to take a vacation from the family or to consciously discuss with the whole family when holiday days are and what can still be done before them.

By delegating work, one can get additional time, and this way a "whatever" day can become another vacation day.

With this system, the feeling of guilt which many people have if they even take a short rest, because they believe that they still have so much to do, is finally gone. Feeling guilty also costs strength and energy. Allow yourself the time in which you do not have anything to do!

With this method you can avoid "unnatural vacation days," which your subconsciousness would otherwise create, for example, with influenza or other illnesses and injuries. It helps you to be healthier, and have more time, more money, and your dreams come true. However, be aware of the other consequences. If you have cleared the victim program, you can't blame others for anything anymore. Are you ready to take responsibility for yourself, your life, and your health?

Healing and Deleting the Victim Program with Archangel Chamuel

If you have taken on the problems of your whole family and other people, it can be helpful for you to do the following meditation with Archangel Chamuel.

- Relax and begin with the Angel Breath (see page 56). Lay your hands on your heart chakra and let the energy flow. Then ask Archangel Chamuel and his helper angels for help deleting the victim program from your life.

- First visualize a big film screen, and on this screen the house or apartment in which you live. Perceive that many angels are present and that everything is illuminated brightly.

- Visualize the angels as they put a very big stove in the center of the house. A big violet flame blazes inside the stove.

- In your visualization, go through the whole house, one room after the other. Everywhere you will see parcels and boxes full of the energetic garbage which you have produced or taken on from others: negative emotions, thought forms, behavior patterns, belief systems, and judgments. The unwanted energies could also be in the form of presents, pictures, furniture, clothes, etc.

- Now take all these packages and boxes and throw them into the stove. Clean one space after the other.

- See how everything is burned in the big stove as the energy is transformed, and how bright white light escapes from the stove and fills the house bit by bit.

- Now ask Archangel Chamuel and his helpers to bring love, joy, luck, health, and freedom into your life. Visualize how Chamuel and the other angels bring this new energy in the form of light balls into your house.

- Look everywhere to see whether the house is really light and bright. If you still discover dark places, ask for revelation and removal of the causes, and then watch how the angels throw these energies in the transformation stove. If the whole house shines in a bright light, the first part of this cleansing process is concluded.

- Visualize the angels removing the big stove and putting a low table with many chairs in the middle of the space. Invite your family members, boss, colleagues, clients, friends, doctors—everyone who has played a role in the victim program—to sit down around this table. As soon as everybody is gathered, announce loudly, *"From this day on, I will never play the victim for anybody. As of today, I choose freedom and allow myself to make my own decisions. Herewith, I release you from the task of showing me my patterns and programs, and I release myself from it."*

- Observe how the persons who are present in your space react. Have they understood? Do they nod their heads?

- Ask all people who understand to leave the space. Should there be a person who does not want to go, ask Chamuel to disconnect and dissolve any karmic connection with this person, and to finally release you from the energy of the victim program.

- Think about how you feel after everyone has left the space. Thank Chamuel, his assistants, and the power of God for their help. Stretch out your arms and say three times, *"I am free. I am free. I am free."*

- Watch the picture on the screen disappear into a sea of golden light. Come back slowly and completely into your body. Before you get up, take some time and then drink a glass of water.

If you sometimes feel like you have fallen back into the habits of the old program, repeat the visualization. (A popular relapse time is the holidays, which are usually spent with family.) In few cases, family members are ready to support the sudden wish for self-realization of a family member (after clearing the victim program), because it is often connected with personal losses of comfort. The usual "service" that most housewives provide for free—like cooking meals, doing laundry, ironing, etc.—could be limited or even lost.

My seventy-five-year-old client Bertha faced some stubborn opposition from her husband when she decided to take part in a weekend seminar for the first time in her life. This decision meant that she could not be there to serve the Sunday pork roast to her husband, which he took for granted every week.

Her husband said, "I do not like this at all!" However, to his surprise, Bertha replied, "Now you finally know how I've felt for over fifty years, when I don't like things that you do." It's never too late to learn or to change!

Chris, fifty-five, had two adult daughters, worked as a nurse, cooked, and spoiled her husband around the clock. She lived the classical victim program, until a sudden accident caused the death of her best friend. This tragedy made her think about her own life.

"Is this all I can do with my life?" she asked herself. She decided soon after to make major changes. She came to my practice and told me about her plan, but she didn't know how she could change her life, because she didn't want to give up her job in the hospice for financial reasons. In our conversation, Chris recognized that subconsciously the victim program was running her life.

She learned the Angel Breath and worked with Archangel Chamuel and her guardian angels on clearing this program. By working with the angels, her true calling and soul purpose became clear to her. Little by little, her life changed. She learned to give back responsibility to her adult daughters, and to accept the help of her husband with household work.

Now she had time for her old, but up until then neglected, passion: herbal healing remedies. Chris got the herbal healing recipes of her mother and grandmother from the basement. She prepared the old family prescriptions for creams and herbal teas, of which she was able to sell a lot. In addition, she offered herbal seminars and nature walks to pass on her valuable knowledge to other people. Chris was able to change her job as a nurse into a part-time position and doubled her monthly income by selling products and seminars. Her new creative task, and the appreciation she got from teaching others, made her very happy and gave her the fulfillment she was always looking for.

CHAPTER 11

The Judge Program

All blame is a waste of time. No matter how much fault you find with another, and regardless of how much you blame him, it will not change you. The only thing blame does is to keep the focus off you when you are looking for external reasons to explain your unhappiness or frustration. You may succeed in making another feel guilty about something by blaming him, but you won't succeed in changing whatever it is about you that is making you unhappy.

—Dr. Wayne Dyer, American author
and inspirational speaker

If you can say with certainty that the victim program does not apply to you at all, then check to see whether the characteristic features of the judge program seem familiar to you.

The judge program has two versions. The first one is marked by the fact that people in this program judge and blame others. Their own dammed-up emotions become the engine for their words and actions. People in this program appear to be very self-confident at first sight. Often they are professionally successful and hold leadership positions. It is very important for them to achieve something in life which also brings material security. They are always busy and very stressed, which becomes apparent, above all, by stomach and heart/circulatory problems.

As children they were good at school or in sports or both. Nevertheless, they felt subconsciously misunderstood and unloved. There was only recognition and love for them if they produced unusual achievements. As adults, they judge people by what they have achieved or by how much money they have. They always try to be better than others, because subconsciously they fear being refused, being alone, and losing.

If other people have not shown any success, in the eyes of the "judges," they are to be punished with disdain or are simply made fun of. People whose lives are run by the judge program are not tolerant toward other cultures, races, and religions. Everything that is different and deviates from their own norm is understood as being hostile.

People with the second version of the judge program blame themselves. They believe they are "not good enough," feel unworthy, have a lack of self-esteem, and tend to have melancholy and depression. They constantly create life situations which contain self-destruction and self-punishment.

Both versions of the judge program can become apparent in a person during different life phases. This often explains the complete breakdown of a person who was always so successful—though only to the outside world.

John was a department manager for a big production company. He was keen, and attended advanced management trainings on a regular basis. He adapted to the newest computer programs easily, and got a salary raise every year. In the classical sense, he was successful, which was shown off to his environment with his new luxury car. He was not liked among his employees, however, because he was known for very unpleasant outbursts of rage.

Anyone who did not live up to John's standards was criticized as a failure. His wife (who lived the victim program) was frightened all the time, and his only son, Steven, had big problems at school. John decided to raise his son very strictly and to discipline him. He wanted to teach him lessons by beating him up. However, Steven could not withstand the pressure of his angry father.

At fifteen, he started to smoke marijuana, and at eighteen, he attempted to commit suicide for the first time. Steven blamed himself (other version of the judge program) because he could not fulfill the expectations of his father, and became depressive.

That same year, John had a heart attack. When the attempted suicide of his son became known within the community and at his work, his personal image as a great father shattered and his whole "perfect world" fell apart.

His wife Elizabeth finally asked me for help, and after John's initial opposition, the whole family came for treatments. After a few Quantum Angel Healing sessions, old emotions, belief systems, and programs were cleared up, and the family's healing process could start. A lot could be transformed with the help of the angels and healed at last.

John was ready to speak about his sore point (the early death of his father), and transformed his need to be the strong hero, as well as his fear of "not being loved" which was emotionally linked to it.

With the help of the angels, Steven, an indigo child, learned to accept his spiritual side and to differentiate himself from his father. He went to Colombia and has worked there, for more than a year now, supporting the Red Cross.

Healing and Deleting the Judge Program with Archangel Jophiel

If you tend to blame others or yourself, the following meditation with Archangel Jophiel can be helpful for you.

- Relax and begin with the Angel Breath (see page 56). Lay your hands on your solar plexus and let the energy flow. Then ask Archangel Jophiel and his assistant angels for support with deleting the judge program.

- Visualize a big film screen with twins—two versions of yourself. The figure on the right shows the dynamic judge's energy and the figure on the left shows the receptive judge's energy. Decide whether one figure is bigger or smaller than the other, more powerful or more weak. Which emotions does one figure hold toward the other? What could the smaller figure need?

- Ask Archangel Jophiel to show you the reason why one figure feels better than the other. Let bright light shine on both figures and ask Archangel Jophiel to remove the root of this program and to transform the energy linked to it.

- Observe how both figures resemble each other more and more in terms of color, size, and dynamics. Ask the dominating judge of your program (dynamic or receptive) whether his mission is finished, or whether there is something else to do.

(For example, observe if files which symbolize the rest of the judge program are thrown away.)

- Thank the dominating judge for his services and tell him that his services are no longer needed and that he can retire now. Watch as this judge relaxes.

- Visualize now how both figures look into each other's eyes and embrace each other. Feel how the love flows between them, and see how they unite and become one single body. Thank God, Jophiel, and his assistants for their help. Feel the love and say three times loudly, *"I love myself. I love myself. I love myself."*

- Watch as the picture on the screen disappears in a sea of golden light. Now slowly and completely come back into your physical body. Take enough time before you get up and drink a glass of water.

From now on, you do not need to blame yourself or others. Remember that the love and the strength of God are present in every person. According to the divine plan, you, and all other people, are already perfect the way you are!

CHAPTER 12

The "Unable to Forgive" Program

The weak can never forgive. Forgiveness is the attribute of the strong.

—*Mahatma Gandhi (1869–1948), spiritual teacher and political leader of India*

Many of us suffer from the results of deep emotional injuries, and it is sometimes difficult to forgive the one that "caused" them. People who are unable to forgive can be resentful, angry, and furious, and thereby suffer even more. In previous chapters of this book, I explained that each of us has created everything in our lives, whether on a more or less conscious level. If it is difficult for you to believe this, and all others are to blame in your eyes, then you are merely the "victim" of circumstances. Please start working on clearing the victim program (see page 67).

If you don't feel like a victim, but are still filled with feelings like rage, fury, hatred, annoyance, grief, or desperation, you should transform this energy for your own well-being, and by doing so, heal yourself. There is a reason why people say things like, "This situation is really getting to me. It's killing me." Painful experiences in personal relationships, when people cannot forgive each other, create energy which has a negative impact on everyone's health.

There is a distinction between people who cannot forgive themselves, and those who cannot forgive other people (they constantly blame others and make them feel guilty). People who feel guilty and helpless tend to be overweight. They often swallow their grief and their feelings of guilt by excessively eating a lot of food. In addition, they often suffer from tonsillitis or discomfort in the digestive tract—or both.

People who blame others tend to have panic attacks and trouble sleeping. They may also articulate their angry emotions by yelling or screaming at others and by insulting them. They tend to be aggressive and nervous, which can lead to colic and inflammation in the body (including endometriosis for women).

Healing and Deleting the "Unable to Forgive" Program with the Archangels Jeremiel and Zadkiel

If you or your client cannot forgive someone, or often feel anger, fury, hatred, annoyance, and grief, the following meditation with the archangels Jeremiel and Zadkiel can be helpful.

- Relax and begin with the Angel Breath. Lay your hands on your second chakra and let the energy flow. Then ask archangels Jeremiel and Zadkiel and the assisting angels for help deleting the "unable to forgive" program.

- Ask the archangels to bring you to your personal healing temple and place of personal power.

Visualize a big hall in this temple and in it a golden throne decorated with different healing and precious stones, on which lies comfortable cushions.

- Take a seat on this throne and breathe deeply in and out. Lay your hands on the armrests and feel how the healing energy flows through you. The energy flows through your whole body and you feel strong. All people (as well as animals and beings) who have hurt you in any form have asked for an audience today. They would like to ask you for forgiveness. They have come from this life and from former lives. Visualize a queue of people and see how one after the other steps before your throne.

- Find time to forgive every single one. Say, *"I forgive you, and with the power of God who I am, I now release all emotions, belief systems, programs, promises, contracts, and energies which were binding us in this life or others."*

- Inhale deeply and visualize how this energy flows out of your energy system and the DNA of every single cell of your body where it was stuck. Archangels Jeremiel and Zadkiel take this energy and put it into golden bowls (transformation vessels). See now how the person before you smiles thankfully and leaves the hall.

- After you forgive every person, envision three versions of yourself standing at the end of the queue. Say to the first body, your mental body, *"I forgive you with the power of God who I am, and I now release all emotions, belief systems, programs, promises, con-*

tracts, and energies which led to self-punishment in this life or others."

- Inhale deeply and visualize how this energy flows out of your energy system and every part of your mental body where it was stuck. Archangels Jeremiel and Zadkiel take this energy and put it into golden bowls. Watch as your mental body steps to the right side of your throne.

- Say to the second body, your emotional body, *"I forgive you with the power of God who I am, and I now release all emotions, belief systems, programs, promises, contracts, and energies which led to self-punishment in this life or others."*

- Inhale deeply and visualize how this energy flows out of your energy system and every part of your emotional body where it was stuck. Archangels Jeremiel and Zadkiel take this energy and put it into golden bowls. Watch as your emotional body steps to the left side of your throne.

- Say to the third body, your physical body, *"I forgive you with the power of God who I am, and I now release all emotions, belief systems, programs, promises, contracts, and energies which led to self-punishment in this life or others."*

- Inhale deeply and visualize how this energy flows out of your energy system and the DNA of every single cell of your body where it was stuck. Archangels Jeremiel and Zadkiel take this energy and put it into golden bowls. Watch as your physical body steps in front of your throne.

- On the throne sits your spiritual body. He asks the other bodies to come forth, embraces them, and melts with them. Now say, *"I forgive myself of everything that I have sworn to never forgive myself for. With the power of God who I am, I now release all emotions, belief systems, programs, promises, contracts, and energies which kept me bound to these oaths, in this life or others."*

- Inhale deeply and visualize how this energy flows out of your energy system and the DNA of every single cell of your body where it was stuck. Archangels Jeremiel and Zadkiel take this energy and put it into golden bowls. Watch as all of the golden transformation bowls are transported out of the hall.

- Watch as the archangels Jeremiel and Zadkiel and the assisting angels applaud and embrace you. Thank them for their help and feel your own strength and the love and gratitude which flow through you. Say, *"I am free. I am free. I am free."*

Let the angels bring you back again. Come back slowly and completely into your body. Rest afterward for several hours. Take enough time to get up and drink at least ten glasses of water; this will help flush your system and clear your physical body. Please note that released emotions can be toxic in your body if they don't get flushed out of your system.

When doing this clearing and healing with a client, keep in mind that the older your client is and the more difficult his life is, the shorter this visualization should be. Sometimes it is enough to fully forgive just one person. This is a very intensive, deep treatment which can last for a long amount of time, depending on the circumstances. The treatment should not be longer than sixty to ninety minutes—for yourself or your clients. If you have not reached the end of the queue after an hour, interrupt the transformation process and continue another day (also for no longer than ninety minutes), until you have reached the end of the line.

At any time, you can go on a new internal journey into your healing temple and personal power place. For example, you may practice this healing exercise if you feel that you have difficulty forgiving someone or if you sense disharmony in your body system.

Dr. B. was of Jewish descent. His parents, brothers, and sisters had died in a concentration camp; he barely survived his time in the camp. With the help of a friend, it was possible for him to flee and emigrate to the United States.

He was a medical doctor, and another doctor referred him to my practice. He had already tried out many alternative healing methods since he had suffered from breathlessness and extreme insomnia for decades. He rarely slept more than two to three hours a night and felt extremely exhausted and lifeless.

The treatment went well. The angels helped him release long-buried emotions and transform them. Dr. B. was very sensitive. He could clearly feel the energy of the angels and saw many colors and light. I was deeply touched and grateful that this almost seventy-year-old man was able to accept the help of the angels after all these years—even if it was very difficult for him to completely forgive.

Two days after the treatment, I called him to find out about his condition. He did not feel good. In fact, he had reacted to the treatment with a fever and skin rashes. I knew that fever was a clear sign of intense transformation and that his skin was reacting to the released emotional energy that had caused him all of those health problems before. My recommendation was to drink more water with lemon juice to support his liver, which was processing all of the toxic energy that had been released. I told him to let me know when he would be ready for the next treatment. It took months until he made the next appointment.

His healing process took a long time; very slowly, he forgave and cured his pains by transforming his buried emotions. I was very grateful to be able to be of service to this man.

CHAPTER 13

The "Love Hurts" Program

If you love somebody, let them go, for if they return, they were always yours. And if they don't, they never were.

—*Kahlil Gibran (1883–1931), Lebanese-American artist, poet, and writer*

Almost all people know from their own experience how heartbreak and the pain of separation feel. If you have felt this way for many years and still think of your ex-partner, or if you experience similar painful situations over and over again, the emotions have expanded into the "love hurts" program which could be very dangerous. This program can lead to depression, heart disease, autoimmune diseases, and cancer. The subconscious emotions of not feeling loved, of feeling abandoned and lonely, are toxic for internal organs. The triggers for this program are often traumatic events, which are like scratches on a record: we do not get over them. Instead, we play the same piece over and over again, whether we want to or not. You can spot the early warning signs of this program in your client by paying attention to how often they speak of a beloved person who has injured them.

A good friend of mine was left by his first love, Katie. For months, he only spoke about Katie. His friends could not stand listening to him crying and complaining about his ex-girlfriend. They made fun of him, and as soon as they saw him they would say, "Hi, Sam. Do you know any sentences that start with a *k*?"

None of the numerous relationships Sam was involved in later on lasted more than a few months. Over and over again, he had the same experience: love hurts. Good-looking Sam is now in his late forties and a successful entrepreneur, but he is still unmarried and has no children. (I hope that he will read this book someday.)

A prerequisite for the successful deletion of the "love hurts" program is the ability to forgive former partner(s) and yourself. Cutting the energetic cords, which can still be there after decades, is also very important.

Healing and Deleting the "Love Hurts" Program with Archangel Raphael

If you can't get over your separation from an ex-partner or have numerous experiences that suggest that "love always hurts," the following visualization with Archangel Raphael can be helpful for you.

- Relax and begin with the Angel Breath (see page 56). Lay your hands on your heart chakra and let the energy flow. Then ask Archangel Raphael and his assistant healing angels for support with the dissolution of the "love hurts" program.

- Close your eyes and visualize a special place that looks like a drive-through car wash. Then read in your mind's eye the sign on the door which says,

"Energetic purification and healing of the 'love hurts' program." Archangel Raphael stands at the door and now asks you to lie down on a comfortable couch. The couch stands on a conveyer belt, which slowly starts moving and takes you through the energetic "car wash." Just relax and enjoy the process while you are lying down comfortably.

- At first, you are transported through a magnetic tunnel. Here, all the energy that has led to this program is removed from the DNA of every single cell and your energy system. The magnetic field in this tunnel is very strong and also removes the energy that you did not want to let go of until now—or were unable to let go of without help. All the energy that you have taken on from other people (knowingly or unknowingly) is removed thoroughly. Visualize how every single cell is cleaned with a special white foam. Remaining etheric cords, which are possibly still attached to you, are also dissolved by this foam and removed for good.

- Next, your couch is automatically transported to the next station. There, you see how Archangel Raphael and his assistants fill green and pink healing balm in every cell of your body and seal the cells. This healing balm consists of pure love energy. It extinguishes all memories of painful situations and brings forth pleasant and loving experiences. Be aware of how internal pictures appear before your spiritual eye. If unpleasant or hurtful memories of certain persons appear, say, **"I forgive you. I release you and send you love."**

- Visualize how your couch moves to the next station, the station of wishes. Everywhere around you are small pink light balls. Feel how you yourself become a magnet and draw these pink light balls toward you as they penetrate your energy body. They enter every cell of your physical body. They contain the magical energy which dreams are made of, and work at the deepest level. They help you have happiness, fulfillment, and love in your life. If you are ready for it, ask Archangel Raphael to help you connect with your most ideal partner, who truly loves you.

- Now you have arrived at the end of the conveyer belt and feel great. You are happy about the new phase of your life which begins now. Get up from the couch and step outside, where you will find yourself in front of a big movie screen. You are seeing the end of a movie. Read the title of the movie: *"I, _____(your name), am happy. I love myself and I am loved."* In the last scene of the movie, you will see the back of yourself. See that you walk hand in hand with your soul mate at the beach. You can only see his back and might not know who he is. The sun is a beautiful golden orange and sets romantically into the sea. Feel how much love and happiness flows through you. You feel safe and loved. Enjoy these feelings for a few more minutes.

- Tell the angels, who are the producers of this film, to roll up the screen. They are happy that you will take over from now on; you are the director and have the leading role in this new film.

- Ask the angels to bring you back. Be assured that the angels work behind the scenes and prepare everything for your new movie, including guiding a wonderful partner to you. You do not need to do anything else—just stay in the energy of love. Now come back completely into your physical body. Feel the joy in your heart and thank the angels for their help.

When Judith, thirty-six, came to see me in my practice, she was crying and felt horrible. Her relationship with her boyfriend made her life a living hell. She was successful in all areas of her life, but in relationships she only experienced disasters. Within four months, she had become the puppet of her new boyfriend, Steven. She couldn't sleep anymore, couldn't eat anymore, was extremely nervous, and only felt good when she was around Steven.

Steven took life easy. His motto was, "We'll see each other around. I'll call you," (though he usually forgot to say when). His attitude and his behavior pushed Judith to her limits. She waited and waited until he finally called. However, in the meantime she had already heard from her friend that Steven had partied with a blond beauty on Saturday night, while she had been sitting next to her phone at home, like a hypnotized rabbit.

Judith longed for a family and a happy future with Steven, but he was a passionate Casanova—unwilling and unable to have a committed relationship. However, Judith could not let go of him. She lost a lot of weight; she weighed not even a hundred pounds. She was in crisis, feeling terribly unloved and deeply hurt.

Judith went through withdrawal like a drug addict, and I explained to her that she had become sexually addicted to Steven; she was addicted to him both emotionally and physically. In the first months of her intense sexual relationship with Steven, Judith's body had poured out a lot of happy hormones, so-called endorphins and other body drugs, that made her feel in love and happy. Whenever she did not hear from Steven, while he was out chasing the next sexual high, Judith reacted with regular withdrawal symptoms.

The angels helped Judith feel calmer and more relaxed. They helped her understand her subconscious "love hurts" program. Her inner child was an injured little girl, who had never felt enough love and appreciation from her daddy. She remembered very well that her father often said to her, "Not now! I have no time for you." Judith often felt pushed away and abandoned. The deep pain of resentment was still very severe inside of her. Later on in life, Judith energetically attracted men who conformed to her "love hurts" program and according belief patterns, which she was not aware of.

Through the dissolution of the "love hurts" program and wonderful inner child healing, Judith was able to develop self-love and acceptance. She cut the energetic cords to Steven and ended the relationship. After a while, Judith had more self-esteem and became stronger and healthy. Six months later, Judith met her future husband, and at the age of thirty-eight, she got pregnant and had two beautiful twin baby girls. Her daughters are growing up with loving parents—and without the "love hurts" program.

CHAPTER 14

The Quantum Angel Healing Formula

A person with a new idea is a crank until the idea succeeds.
—Mark Twain (1835–1910), American author,
journalist, and humorist

As I already explained in preceding chapters, the angels do not interfere with our free will. However, they can help us find the causes for our problems and illnesses, and help cure them if we are ready. By the law of resonance (explained in the introduction), the oscillation frequency of our body and our energy field changes during the healing process described below. The angels and their high-energy energy field support us, since we resonate with the field.

The intensity of the QAH energy treatment is much higher than the intensity of energy treatments by human practitioners who only use their own energy source. With QAH, detrimental and harmful energies can be transformed in the DNA of every single cell. It is important to transform possible blocking emotions on a regular basis, before limiting belief systems and serious programs can form.

Eva-Maria Mora

Even if emotions have not yet expanded into harmful programs, they can strongly influence our health. Fears can develop, for example, into phobias, which are often enhanced by excessive consumption of sweets and coffee. Emotions and associated belief systems can be responsible for whether we succeed or fail, have money or not, or fail or fulfill our real purpose in this life.

The purpose of this healing work is to activate the memory of the perfect blueprint of the cell and raise its vibration to the original program of perfect health and love.

The most important steps of the Quantum Angel Healing formula are:

- Opening yourself to the flow of angelic healing energies

- Forgiving (If you have difficulty forgiving yourself or others, please refer to the "unable to forgive" program on pages 177 ff.)

- Letting go of and transforming old emotions and harmful energies

- Visualizing

- Accepting love, new energies, and new belief systems

- Feeling gratitude

This formula has several variables and can therefore be tailor-made to your specific situation or those of your clients.

To begin, ask God to send you his love and healing energy. You can also specifically ask for the assistance of beings of light who you are familiar with and who you trust (angels, spirit guides, etc.). Determine the emotions which you want to transform, as well as the emotions which you would like to have instead.

If you have raised your frequency by energetic clearing and the Angel Breath, and you are ready to be in contact with the angels, say from the bottom of your heart (or let your client say from the bottom of their heart):

"I ask the power of God and the angel [insert angel's name, e.g., Raphael, here] *to find and delete the cause of my* [insert the emotion you would like to transform, e.g., "fear of failure," here] *which was stored in my being and my DNA, in this or a former life.*

(Here, I also mean the God power within ourselves and within all that is.)

"I ask that all other emotions, thoughts, programs, and energies—which I am unaware of and which caused this situation or illness—are transformed now."

(Wait a few minutes. The cause may be shown to you as one picture or message or many; however, this is not necessary for the success of the treatment. It is possible that you will perceive roots or energy clouds, which are released from your energy body and the DNA of your cells.)

"I forgive myself and everyone connected to the origin of this situation. I let go of the emotions, energy, and programs linked with it for good."

(Take two to three deep breaths and exhale slowly. Visualize how all cells of the energy body and the DNA open up, and the old stored energy leaves.)

"I ask for transformation and healing for good of all aspects of my being at all levels, physical, mental, emotional, and spiritual, in all situations, dimensions, and universes."

(Visualize the cells filling with life force energy in the form of white light.)

"Now I accept unconditional love for myself and choose from now on for my life _____ [Fill in the blank here,

always using "I feel" or "I am" statements. For example, you could say, "I feel powerful"; "I am cured"; or "I am healthy."].

(Visualize an iridescent, clear energy cloud with white, green, blue, gold, and pink light, which wraps around you and your new creation and seals you.)

"With all my heart, I thank the power and grace of God and the angels for their help!"

(Feel how love and gratitude flows through you, and feel the peace, calmness, joy, and happiness inside you. Your physical body might feel warm and pleasant as well. You are in alignment with your soul purpose. You are in balance and harmony).

Using the Quantum Angel Healing Formula

You can use the QAH formula for self-healing or to support the healing of your client. Always begin by writing down the emotions of your client that possibly led to the illness or difficult life situation (refer to part 2 of this book for a list of illnesses and symptoms). Double-check the client's belief system, and ask the client if they are ready to heal (explained on page 8). Decide which helpful emotions and thoughts the client should substitute for the negative emotions which need to be transformed.

Next, write down the precise text of the suitable healing formula and slowly lead your client through the transformation process. During the treatment, allow the angelic energy to flow through your channel (explained in chapter 4) and into your hands. Lay your hands on the area of the body which needs to be treated or the chakra which is connected to the problem (see page xx). If the treatment is for emotional healing, lay your hands on the front and the back of the heart chakra; we call this the "sandwich" hand position. Always make sure that the energy flows back and forth between your hands to build an energy circuit.

Trust your intuition and the guidance of the angels. Let the angel's energy flow in through your energy channel and out through your hands, for fifteen minutes or longer. Have some tissues available since the emotions may be released as tears. Strong fear is also released through the liquid of the nasal mucous membrane and the sinuses. It is very likely that your client will feel the impact of the treatment immediately. They may sense it physically, e.g., sensing warmth and tingling energy, or visually, e.g., seeing light and colors.

Because the healing energies of the angels also impact the energy system and body of the QAH practitioner, healing will also take place at the same time for you. It is possible that so-called angel tears may flow out of the corners of your eyes, without you feeling any emotions attached to them. It is also possible that you may have the urge to yawn repeatedly. Both reactions indicate that a transformation and clearing process is taking place. This is similar to what happens in an airplane before landing; it is just an adjustment and pressure release. Explain to your client before the treatment that you are not tired, but merely function as a channel through which energy is transformed.

If you can sense that your client is very blocked, let the energy flow through you for approximately forty-five minutes or even an hour. Just be sure your hands lay on the patient's body with very little weight; your hands should feel as light as the wings of a butterfly to your patient. If you receive pictures and messages from the angels, share them with your client during or after the energy treatment. Ask the client if they received any messages or saw any pictures. Very often, both the client and the practitioner see the same images, just like two television sets that receive the same broadcast. Be sensitive and compassionate when you speak with your client; allow the angels to help you find the right wording. They might give you more pictures or metaphors when you speak to your client, to make it easier for the client to understand their message. If you receive unpleasant images during the treatment and the angels do not repeat them, there is no need to discuss them since they were simply old energies that were being cleared. (If you help someone clean their house, you don't discuss the contents of their garbage can afterward.) Focus on the new energies and new emotions and speak about the beautiful new life that just started.

After the treatment, a clear difference of well-being will be noticeable. Peace, joy, happiness, and gratitude are typical felt emotions, as is relief from pressure and pain. (This is also the case, if you—as an experienced QAH practitioner—guide your clients over the telephone. The angels treat them wherever they are.)

Give your client a glass of water and the chance to rest a little. Make sure they are grounded and feeling really good before they leave your practice and maybe drive a car.

If this is your client's first treatment with you and the angels, it is advisable to work on only one subject, symptom, or emotion. Clients who are in difficult life situations might need more treatments, often for several different subjects. Before they leave, ask your client to call you in a few days at a time that's convenient for both of you, so you can find out how they are doing. If necessary, offer to be available for another appointment. Listen to your own intuition and let the angels guide you. Never offer a ten-session package or such, up front. This is not suitable for this kind of work; you never know how fast a client can heal and what miracles will happen during a QAH treatment.

If you work with a client on an issue with their father, for example, it's absolutely possible that their relationship with their husband will also change for the better afterward. Or, you could treat a client for certain emotional problems, whereupon their skin heals and becomes more beautiful. These are so-called emotional chain reactions. If the cause of a problem is transformed, all symptoms and subjects linked to it clear up as well.

If you work on yourself, record the tailor-made healing formula, so that you are not in the head, but in the heart, during this work. Lay your hands on your heart chakra or, depending on the symptom, another chakra. Make sure that you sit or lie down comfortably. If you want to treat physical problems, you can also lay your hands directly on an aching body part, provided that this is easily feasible. Let the energy flow for a minimum of fifteen minutes, or until you have the feeling that the treatment is complete.

It is possible that you will feel very light afterward or that your whole body will feel different. Get up slowly, drink a glass of water, and rest.

Self-Rejection

After working with clients for many years, I have found that almost every person subconsciously rejects themselves. This rejection can refer to one single area or to a lot of areas. It seems that everyone has at least one thing which they do not like about themselves. People feel stupid, overweight, unattractive, incapable, etc. Watch out for people who state that they don't have any problems or weaknesses, and always feel the need to tell others how wonderful, talented, and special they are.

If you would like to transform self-rejection into self-acceptance and self-love, which is necessary for good health, you could use the Quantum Angel Healing formula which follows. (Please include the instructions and visualizations of the original formula on pages 193 ff. as well. Breathe, and feel the flow of the energies!)

"I ask the power of God within and Archangel Michael to find and to remove the origin and the roots of the negative emotion 'I feel fat,' which was stored in my DNA in this or a former life. I ask that all other subconscious emotions, thoughts, belief systems, programs, and energies that caused me to feel this way [or caused this condition] are now transformed. I forgive myself and everyone who played a role in creating this feeling [or condition], and let go of the related energies and programs for good. I ask for transformation and healing of all aspects of my being, in all directions of time and space, in all dimensions and universes. I now accept for myself unconditional love and choose the emotion, 'I like and accept myself the way I am. I feel beautiful, slim, and attractive. I am worthy of being loved, including by myself.'

"With all my heart, I thank the power of God and the angels for their help."

Resistance

The first step in changing a situation is accepting that our real "enemies" are inside ourselves. These are our suppressed emotions, which we often are unaware of. Once you have accepted this and stop resisting or denying these emotions, you can work constructively on yourself. This resistance is like an iron ball which is chained to your ankle. Only when you accept what is can you change something and become free at last. To support your transformation process, you can visualize Archangel Michael releasing the chains around your neck, as well as around your wrists and ankles, that held you prisoner of your own emotions.

Finish the visualization with the words, *"I am free. I am free. I am free."*

Lack of Self-Confidence

Another widespread issue is a lack of self-confidence, which can often leave people unable to achieve anything. A lack of self-confidence can also be looked at as a symptom. The underlying emotion might be on a deeper, hidden level and can be transformed with a suitable QAH formula. For example, you could write, "I ask the power of God within and Archangel Jophiel to find and remove the roots of the emotions that keep me from trusting myself and from being self-confident." Work through as instructed, then write, "I believe in myself, I trust myself and my abilities, and I feel safe and self-confident with everything I do."

Fear of Failure

A fear of failure includes all emotions that are connected to doubting your own success and the effectiveness of what you do, including your work with the QAH formula or other tools. As long as these doubts remain and the attached energies are not transformed, we create situations of self-sabotage. The emotional program always wins over the good intentions, and the limiting belief systems will always be right like they have been in the past. Write a suitable healing formula and use it. For example, "I ask the power of God within and Archangel Azrael to find and remove the cause of the emotions that make me fail and do not allow me to do what I want to do." Allow the process to occur, and then fill in the blanks, "I feel my success. I feel the accomplishment of what I intended to do. I feel the effects and results of my new success program in all areas of my life."

What Is Blocking My Success?

Your self-confidence will be strengthened by the application of the tailor-made healing formula, but the formula will not necessarily clear everything which stood in the way of your success until now. Continue to pay attention to your emotions, as well as to your thoughts. There may be even more that negatively affects the success of certain plans. If you become aware of negative and limiting thoughts and emotions, use the healing formula, and keep transforming those thoughts and emotions and replace them with new positive emotions.

Our DNA is like the hard drive of a supercomputer, on which programs are stored, as well as folders and single documents. If you have trouble extinguishing a certain program, work step by step through all folders (emotions) and documents (belief systems and patterns).

With the help of the following case studies from my practice, you can check your own emotions and belief systems regarding the popular issue of "having financial success." With these clients, the purification and transformation of their emotional patterns have considerably contributed to their financial success and brought measurable results.

Tanya told me, "I am not worthy of having a lot of money. I do not deserve to have things go well for me." She worked with Archangel Gabriel and transformed her emotions with the healing formula: "I am worthy of having a lot of money, and I deserve financial freedom." Within three months of our session, she found a publisher for her children's book and received royalties for her book sales.

Andrea worked as a volunteer in third-world countries for a charity organization. She told me, "I am unable to accept money, as long as there are poor people in other countries." She worked with Archangel Uriel and transformed her emotions with the healing formula: "I am grateful for the money that comes to me. I have great success with my projects." For the next Christmas charity event, Andrea was able to collect many donations. A lot more money was donated than in the years before. She was chosen by her charity organization to fly to Africa and to help on-site with the construction of a school and boarding house for children.

Caroline was really afraid of money. During her childhood, she had experienced her father's devastating gambling addiction, which caused a lot of harm to her family. He often took money that her mother put away to buy groceries for gambling, and because of it, many nights there was no food on the table.

She was afraid of becoming like her father and told me, "I have fear of financial success. I would only lose the money through gambling." She asked Archangel Raphael for help and transformed her emotions with the healing formula: "I choose financial success for my life and spend my money wisely." Caroline received deep transformational healing and interestingly benefited from the money that her boyfriend won through gambling. With the money, they bought a condominium and went on a three-month trip to New Zealand.

John was a jobless architect. He told me, "I am not good enough to find a well-paid job." Then he worked with Archangel Jeremiel and transformed his emotions with the healing formula: "I feel good enough to earn a lot of money. I know I will be guided to find my dream job." Shortly thereafter, John received an offer to work in Japan for two years. A Japanese businessman wanted to build an exact copy of a German castle. John happily accepted the offer as project manager and met his future wife in Japan.

Barbara was a bitter person and jealous of everyone who had a better education than she had. These unresolved emotions caused conflicts in her life. She'd had difficulties at all of her previous jobs and was unemployed when she came to me. She asked Archangel Jophiel to find the roots of the emotions and to remove those "which cause my jealousy and my resentment of successful people." She chose the healing formula: "I am happy for everyone who has success, and I feel successful myself." She got hired as a secretary and worked for an educational institution where people who flunked out of school have another chance to get their high school diploma.

Julian was dyslexic and had major difficulties at school. His father was the CEO of a big financial institution. In spite of his son's bad grade point average, he "helped" his son get a job in a bank. It was unavoidable that his son failed at the job and was fired. Julian said, "I am ashamed. I am not smart enough. I will fail at everything that I try."

He worked with his guardian angel and a whole angel team, which he called the "success angels," and chose the healing formula: "I am confident. I am successful at work. Every day I have more and more success. I am abundant." To the surprise of his father, Julian went to culinary school and got a job as a cook on a big cruise ship. He traveled far away from home, saw the world, and was honored for his creative desserts. He plans to open a restaurant in the near future.

Stephanie had a healing practice for animals, but business was very slow for her. Every month she was worried about whether she would have enough income to pay the rent for her practice. After one year, she was not able to pay the rent anymore, and hoped her clients would bring their animals for treatment to her apartment. This caused problems with her landlord. Stephanie said, "When I am poor, I am closer to God. It is not good to receive money for spiritual healing work." After I explained the principle of energy exchange to her, Stephanie asked Archangel Ariel for help and chose the solution formula: "I am grateful for my financial success. It is a blessing which enables me to do more good for myself and others." After this treatment, Stephanie accepted a temporary job at a well-known pet store. There, she met many animal lovers. She talked to them about her healing work and soon got new clients. In the evening hours, she did in-house visits for sick animals. Just by word of mouth, she got very busy and earned good money. She was able to buy a new car, which allowed her to drive around town and help even more animals.

The Principle of Equalizing Energy Flows

Stephanie is a good example of many dedicated healers who surely mean well, but do neither themselves nor their clients a favor by refusing to accept adequate pay for their work. My teacher Zohar has explained to me that many people have a problem accepting something, for example, money, presents, compliments, etc., for their work.

As healing practitioners, we expect that our clients are able to accept the important information and healing energy which are helpful for them. However, if we give the treatment free of charge, we make it needlessly difficult for them to accept the energies. As soon as we charge, we open an energetic door, and the exchanged energies can flow back and forth.

Have you ever heard, "If this is so expensive, it must be good" or "If this is so cheap, it can't be good"? Make it clear that your work is very valuable. In reality, good health and happiness are priceless.

Of course, your hourly rate should be adequate. If you want to know how much it is, ask your angels. Pay attention to signs and messages relating to your hourly rates. If your clients express several times that your work is too expensive, you should double-check to see if you indeed are greedy, or if you still have unworthiness issues that are being mirrored to you by your clients. If your clients regularly offer you more money than you have asked for, it is time to raise your hourly rates. If you don't, you will soon have less clients than before, and not vice versa. If the angels give you a salary raise, you should accept it!

You will probably also have clients who really have no money. Do not shame these people by working free of charge; instead, accept another form of energy exchange for your treatment (e.g., a haircut, a picture, a cake, babysitting, etc.).

"Give a man a fish and you feed him for a day. Teach a man to fish and you feed him for a lifetime."

It can be interesting to figure out your emotions and programs concerning money. As soon as you become clear, everything will work out just fine.

How Does the Quantum Angel Healing Formula Work?

Emotional blockades and programs often give us the feeling of standing in front of a wall, which gets bigger and bigger the closer we get to it. Emotional blockades are the stones, and energy is the mortar which holds the stones in place.

If you apply the QAH formula to individual emotions, it is like clearing away a wall, one stone at a time. Sometimes, you clear away a whole wall and find the next one behind it. Please do not be discouraged; just keep on working through it. However, other times, there is no big wall, but just a few stumbling blocks on your path. In either case, the more often you apply the QAH formula, the more stones you remove from your path, and the more transformation takes place.

By raising your frequency with the help of the angels, stuck energy is released from your energy bodies and all cells. Blocking and limiting walls can collapse quickly, so that vitality and love can flow freely again, and you can get the results which you truly desire.

Through entrainment with the high frequency of the angels' energy and transformation of the blocking energy, physical, emotional, mental, and spiritual healing takes place. The conflict between thoughts and emotions is resolved. You are more in power and you have more internal balance. You develop more compassion, empathy, and love for yourself and others. You have an antidote for all difficult situations and every illness.

You can help yourself and others. Another benefit you gain by working the QAH formula is that your energy body and your chakra system clears more and more. This makes it easier for you to receive and pass on the messages of the angels and their healing energies.

Part 2

Illnesses and Symptoms

It is not enough to know, one has to apply it. It is not enough to want it, one has to do it.

—*Johann Wolfgang von Goethe (1749–1832),*

German poet

The following list of illnesses and symptoms, which might be caused by suppressed emotions, limiting belief systems, or subconscious programs, is not meant to be complete. I do not claim that the listed illnesses or symptoms are only caused by these emotions or programs. You might find additional or other related emotions within yourself or your client. Every person is a unique individual and therefore has developed individual symptoms for different reasons. Children usually do not develop deep programs until they are twelve years or older, but they often suffer from suppressed emotions. Please understand that neither QAH nor anyone or anything else can cure illnesses. All healing is self-healing which can only be supported. Nevertheless, experience shows that the transformation of emotional energy can lead to successful self-healings. To work with this list, please look at the symptom and probable emotion/program, if it resonates with you apply the QAH formula with the suggested hand position and angels accordingly. If it does not resonate with you, proof first if you are in denial, and then find out, with the help of the angels, if other buried emotions/belief systems/programs are connected to the symptom and apply the QAH formula.

The four major subconscious programs are:

1. Love hurts program
2. Victim program
3. Unable to forgive program
4. Judge program

While running energy, you may put your hands directly on the organ or corresponding chakra. You may then work with the Quantum Angel Healing formula and visualizations to delete the specific programs. With a little practice, you can become aware of the personalized instructions of the angels. Listen carefully and follow the divine guidance.

Abscess
Programs and emotions:
Wants revenge
Rage
Stagnation
Can't let go
Can't forgive
Hand positions: first chakra
Deletion: judge program
Archangels: Sandalphon, Jophiel

Acne
Programs and emotions:
Feels guilty
Lacks self-love
Feels negative toward him/herself
Can't approve/accept (not even her/himself)
Can't accept reality
Hand positions: first chakra
Deletion: unable to forgive program
Archangels: Raphael, Sandalphon

Addictions
Programs and emotions:
Feels alone
Feels excluded
Feels guilt/guilty
Flees the present and the past

Lacks self love
Hand positions: fourth chakra
Deletion: victim program
Archangel: Chamuel

Aggression, aggressive behavior
Programs and emotions:
Feels as though others do not understand her/him
Feels treated unjustly
Suppressed anger, fury, and rage
Does not grant mercy to anyone
Does not grant mercy to him/herself (auto-aggression)
Feels hatred
Deep emotional pain, fear
Hand positions: first and second chakras
Deletion: unable to forgive program
Archangels: Gabriel, Raphael, Sandalphon, Jeremiel, Zadkiel

Aging, problems with
Programs and emotions:
Can't accept the current situation
Struggles with the past
Prefers to blame others
Fears being her/himself
Fears own God power
Hand positions: third chakra
Deletion: judge program
Archangels: Raphael, Michael, Uriel, Jophiel

AIDS
Programs and emotions:
Feels left alone
Feels defenseless and hopeless

Deeply rooted rage
Does not feel good enough
Lacks self-love
Feels negatively toward him/herself
Can't approve/accept (not even her/himself)
Hand positions: third and fourth chakras
Deletion: victim program
Archangels: Raphael, Michael, Uriel, Chamuel

Allergies

Programs and emotions:
Feels defenseless, unprotected, desperate
Does not accept own (God) power
Suppressed mourning
Feels burdened by others or him/herself
Fears opening up emotionally
Fears being hurt
Fears being able to do what he/she would like
Hand positions: third and fourth chakras
Deletion: victim program
Archangels: Haniel, Michael, Raphael, Uriel, Chamuel

Alzheimer's Disease

Programs and emotions:
Suppressed rage, anger
Feels unable to keep his/her own life under control
Feels insecure and/or inferior
Feels helpless and hopeless
Wants to live in his/her own little world
Does not want to adapt
Hand positions: second and third chakras
Deletion: victim program
Archangels: Gabriel, Raphael, Chamuel

Amnesia
Programs and emotions:
Feels guilty
Fears the future
Fears expressing his/her own opinion
Tends to flee/escape
Hand positions: third chakra
Deletion: victim program
Archangels: Michael, Raphael, Uriel, Chamuel

Anemia
Programs and emotions:
Lacks self-love
Does not feel good enough
Lacks the ability to feel joy
Manipulates and controls others
Fears that life does not work out as she/he would like
Fears getting hurt
Hand positions: fourth and seventh chakras
Deletion: victim program
Archangels: Chamuel and Metatron

Anal problems
Programs and emotion:
Anxiety about surviving, external threat
Feels helpless and weak
Can't let go
Can't forgive
Hand positions: first chakra
Deletion: unable to forgive program
Archangels: Raphael, Sandalphon

Anorexia
Programs and emotions:
Rejects her/himself
Lacks self-love
Self-hate
Self-destruction
Self-doubt
Feels unable to satisfy parents (often the mother)
Feels generally unable to live up to expectations
Ignorant of his/her own God power
Hand positions: third and fourth chakras
Deletion: victim program
Archangels: Michael, Raphael, Uriel, Chamuel

Apathy
Programs and emotions:
Self-doubt, self-abandonment
Wishes to escape to another world
Longs for spirituality, love, and security
Suppressed creativity
Fears authority and control
Hand positions: fourth and sixth chakras
Deletion: victim program
Archangels: Raziel, Chamuel

Arteriosclerosis
Programs and emotions:
Feels under pressure
Feels restricted
Feels as though others do not understand her/him
Can't forgive others
Resistant to parents or superiors
Fears punishment

Hand positions: fourth chakra
Deletion: unable to forgive program
Archangels: Chamuel, Jeremiel, Zadkiel

Arthritis
Programs and emotions:
Criticizes him/herself and others
Is judgmental, dogmatic
Can't let go
Can't forgive
Feels depressive, frightened, unloved
Suppressed anger, rage
Rigid beliefs and programs
Fears change
Hand positions: fourth chakra
Deletion: victim program, unable to forgive program
Archangels: Chamuel, Jeremiel, Zadkiel

Arthrosis
Programs and emotions:
Feels helpless and unable to change life
Suppressed mourning and rage
Inner conflict: emotions and thoughts are contrary
Lacks trust in her/himself and others
Hand positions: fourth chakra
Deletion: victim program
Archangel: Chamuel

Asthma
Programs and emotions:
Suppressed childhood fears coming to life again
Desires security and protection
Feels dominated by a parent
Suppressed problems and tears

Is neither happy with his/her own life situation nor with her/himself
Prefers looking back rather than looking forward
Hand positions: fourth chakra
Deletion: victim program
Archangels: Chamuel, Raphael

Asthma in children
Programs and emotions:
Fears being left alone
Does not understand why he/she is on earth
Hand positions: fourth chakra
Deletion: victim program
Archangels: Chamuel, Raphael

Autoimmune diseases
Programs and emotions:
Feels helpless
Feels that the life situation is too much for her/him
Laughs outwardly but cries inside
Deep pain and mourning
Hand positions: fourth chakra
Deletion: victim program
Archangels: Azrael, Chamuel

Back pain, general
Programs and emotions:
Excessive burdens
Lacks support
Frustration
Carries too much responsibility
Rejects further responsibility
Hand positions: put hand on back directly where pain is and "sandwich" with other hand

Deletion: locate the pain (upper, middle, lower) and delete accordingly with specified angels

back pain, upper
Programs and emotions:
Feels unloved
Feels guilt from the past
Deletion: victim program
Archangels: Raphael, Chamuel, Zadkiel

back pain, middle
Programs and emotions:
Lack of self- love
Lacks a feeling of his/her own value
Can't let go of the past
Deletion: unable to forgive program
Archangels: Jeremiel, Zadkiel, Michael, Uriel

back pain, lower
Programs and emotions:
Feels unfree
Lacks financial support
Existential fear
Painful relationship/family situation
Would rather run away, but can't
Deletion: love hurts program
Archangels: Raphael, Sandalphon, Gabriel

Bed-wetting
Programs and emotions:
Fears parents (often the father)
Fears punishment
Hand positions: first and sixth chakras

Deletion: victim program
Archangels: Chamuel, Sandalphon, Raziel

Blood pressure, high
Programs and emotions:
Suppressed rage and anger
Judges others
Is afraid of not being able to fulfill demands
Is desperate
Hand positions: first and fourth chakras
Deletion: judge program
Archangels: Jophiel, Sandalphon, Chamuel

Blood pressure, low
Programs and emotions:
Feels unloved
Depressed
Self-doubts
Gives him/herself up for lost
Hand positions: first and fourth chakras
Deletion: victim program
Archangels: Chamuel

Blood problems
Lacks self-love
Little zest/lust for life
Can't let go
Stagnation
Hand positions: first and fourth chakras
Deletion: victim program
Archangels: Sandalphon, Chamuel

Bone problems
Programs and emotions:
Feels rejected, but suppresses this feeling
Feels separated (from God, from partner)
Feels treated unjustly
Feels under pressure and rebels
Inner rebellion
Hand positions: fourth and fifth chakras
Deletion: victim program
Archangels: Chamuel, Zadkiel

Brain diseases
Programs and emotions:
Feels unable to control own life
Feels stressed and put under pressure
Is nervous
Hand positions: sixth and seventh chakras
Deletion: unable to forgive program
Archangels: Chamuel, Raziel, Metatron

brain tumor
Programs and emotions:
Unable to get involved in new things
Unable to let go of old belief systems
Unable to forgive
Suppressed emotional injuries
Lacks self-love
Hand positions: sixth and seventh chakras
Deletion: unable to forgive program, victim program, love hurts program
Archangels: Chamuel, Raphael, Raziel, Metatron

meningitis
Programs and emotions:
Feels to know it all
Not open-minded
Hand positions: sixth and seventh chakras
Deletion: unable to forgive program
Archangels: Chamuel, Raziel, Metatron, Jeremiel, Zadkiel

Breast problems
Programs and emotions:
Conflict with one's feeling of his/her own value
No self-love
In conflict when having to mother or feed others
Hand positions: fourth chakra
Deletion: victim program, love hurts program
Archangels: Chamuel, Raphael

Breathing difficulties
Programs and emotions:
Unable to come close to people
Can't accept/approve
Feels unworthy
Feels guilt
Self-denial
No trust in others (family)
Hand positions: fourth chakra
Deletion: victim program, love hurts program
Archangels: Chamuel, Raphael

Bronchitis
Programs and emotions:
Extreme disagreement in the family

Wishes to change but at the same time feels discouragement
Unsatisfied longing for harmony and peace
Hand positions: fifth chakra
Deletion: love hurts program
Archangels: Raphael, Chamuel, Zadkiel

Bulimia
Programs and emotions:
Can't accept her/himself
No self-love
Unsatisfied need for love
Feels stressed by expectations of others
Self-destruction
Self-doubts
Longs for spiritual growth
Hand positions: third and fourth chakras
Deletion: victim program, love hurts program
Archangels: Raphael, Chamuel

Burns
Programs end emotions:
Feels defenseless
Feels treated unjustly
Disharmony in one's own life situation
Suppressed rage
Hand positions: all chakras
Deletion: victim program
Archangels: Sandalphon, Michael, Raphael, Uriel, Azrael, Chamuel, Jeremiel, Zadkiel, Metatron, Raziel, Gabriel

Burping
Programs and emotions:
Is mad at him/herself and others
Feels separated
Fears missing something important
Fears being excluded, overseen, or neglected
Hand positions: fourth chakra
Deletion: victim program
Archangels: Chamuel

Cancer
Programs and emotions:
Lacks self-love
Lacks feeling of self-worth
Self-destruction
Deep emotional wounds (also from his/her parents)
Suppressed anger, hate
Can't forgive and is desperate
Feels suppressed
Feels helpless/hopeless
Unconscious death wish
Hand positions: fourth chakra
Deletion: victim program, unable to forgive program, love hurts program
Archangels: Michael, Raphael, Uriel, Chamuel

Cellulitis
Programs and emotions:
Feels guilty
Feels unfree
Can't forgive
Hand positions: first, second, and fourth chakras
Deletion: victim program, unable to forgive program

Archangels: Sandalphon, Chamuel, Zadkiel, Jeremiel, Gabriel, Raphael

Cholesterol level, too high
Programs and emotions:
Feels unhappy
Feels unfree
Feels unworthy of having and perceiving joy
Fears perceiving joy
Hand positions: fourth chakra
Deletion: victim program
Archangels: Chamuel

Chronic pain
Programs and emotions:
Feels unloved
Feels left alone
Seeks support
Looks for the sense of life
Hand positions: third chakra
Deletion: victim program
Archangels: Raphael, Michael, Uriel, Chamuel

Circulatory disorders
Programs and emotions:
Feels overstretched
Doesn't like his/her work
Feels tense
Feels discouraged
Hand positions: fourth chakra
Deletion: victim program
Archangels: Raphael, Chamuel

Cold

Programs and emotions:
Feels uncomfortable at work and at home
Feels confused
Feels misunderstood
Feels illnesses belong to life
Hand positions: fourth and seventh chakras
Deletion: victim program
Archangels: Raphael, Chamuel, Metatron

Colic

Programs and emotions:
Feels confused and stressed
Bottled up rage
Lacks patience
Anger due to/about own life situation
Hand positions: third and fourth chakras
Deletion: judge program
Archangels: Michael, Raphael, Uriel, Chamuel, Jophiel

Constipation

Programs and emotions:
Can't let go of old belief systems and emotions
Feels misunderstood
Resistant to flow of life
Fears not being loved
Hand positions: first, second, third, and fourth chakras
Deletion: victim program, unable to forgive program
Archangels: Sandalphon, Gabriel, Raphael, Michael, Uriel, Chamuel, Jeremiel, Zadkiel

Coughing
Programs and emotions:
Feels misunderstood
Feels unloved
Can't express own needs
Hand positions: third and fourth chakras
Deletion: love hurts program, victim program
Archangels: Raphael, Michael, Uriel, Chamuel

Cramps
Programs and emotions:
Feels treated unjustly
Resistant to authority
Conflict between thoughts and emotions
Can't let go
Can't forgive
Hand positions: first and fourth chakras
Deletion: victim program, unable to forgive program
Archangels: Sandalphon, Chamuel, Jeremiel, Zadkiel

Cystitis
Programs and emotions:
Disharmony in partnership
Feels as though others do not understand her/him sexually
Feels sexually stressed/excessive demand
Hand positions: first chakra
Deletion: love hurts program
Archangels: Raphael, Sandalphon

Cysts
Programs and emotions:
Feels unloved

Grief coming from childhood
Unfulfilled desire to have children
Hand positions: second, fourth, and fifth chakras
Deletion: victim program, love hurts program
Archangels: Chamuel, Raphael, Zadkiel, Gabriel

Deafness
Programs and emotions:
Feels excluded
Feels rejected
Fears changes
Hand positions: fifth and sixth chakras
Deletion: love hurts program
Archangels Raphael, Chamuel, Zadkiel, Raziel

Dental problems
Programs and emotions:
Indecision
Lacks ability to make decisions
Delays decisions

maxilla (upper jaw)
Doesn't understand his/her own life situation

mandible (lower jaw)
Restlessness, impatience
Hand positions: fourth and fifth chakras
Deletion: victim program, unable to forgive program
Archangels: Chamuel, Jeremiel, Zadkiel

periodontitis
Programs and emotions:
Feels forced to make decisions
Can't finish things

Hand positions: fourth and fifth chakras
Deletion: victim program, love hurts program
Archangels: Chamuel, Raphael, Zadkiel

root of the tooth, problems
Programs and emotions:
Lack of support
Excessive stress
Seeks new hold
Hand positions: fourth and fifth chakras
Deletion: victim program, love hurts program
Archangels: Chamuel, Raphael, Zadkiel

Deposits
Programs and emotions:
Hard on him/herself
Wants to be perfect
Fears disappointment
Feels inhibited
Hand positions: fourth chakra
Deletion: judge program
Archangels: Chamuel, Jophiel

Depression
Programs and emotions:
Feels hopeless
Feels helpless
Feels powerless
Feels as if she/he is not good enough
Self-abandonment
Suppressed anger with her/himself
Hand positions: third chakra
Deletion: love hurts program
Archangels: Raphael, Michael, Uriel

Diabetes
Programs and emotions:
Judges self and others
Is disappointed in life
Deep sorrow
Unprocessed emotional shock
Extreme need for control
Is embarrassed by past events
Hand positions: third chakra
Deletion: judge program, unable to forgive program
Archangels: Michael, Raphael, Uriel, Jophiel, Jeremiel, Zadkiel

Diarrhea
Programs and emotions:
Fears something in the present
Wish to separate from someone or something
Wish to run away
Refusal of something which cannot be accepted
Fears own rejection/disapproval
Hand positions: first and second chakras
Deletion: victim program
Archangels: Raphael, Chamuel, Gabriel

Dysentery
Programs and emotions:
Restlessness
Fears present
Rage and anger
Can't forgive
Hand positions: first and fourth chakras
Deletion: unable to forgive program
Archangels: Jeremiel, Zadkiel, Sandalphon, Chamuel

Ear problems
Programs and emotions:
Has the feeling that no one listens to him/her
Doesn't listen to his/her own inner voice
Feels disharmony in personal environment
Rage and anger
Resistance to change
Resistant to innovation
Hand positions: fifth and sixth chakras
Deletion: love hurts program
Archangels: Raphael, Chamuel, Zadkiel, Raziel

Eczema
Programs and emotions:
Strong emotions
Hypersensitive
Unhealed emotional pain, irritation
Feels frustrated
Hand positions: third and fourth chakras
Deletion: victim program
Archangels: Michael, Raphael, Uriel, Chamuel

Elbows, problems with
Programs and emotions:
Can't accept new experiences
Fears changes
Hand positions: third and fourth chakras
Deletion: unable to forgive program
Archangels: Michael, Raphael, Uriel, Chamuel, Jeremiel, Zadkiel

Endometriosis
Programs and emotions:
Deep and not released sadness
Frustration
Insecurity
Lacks self love
Lacks self-awareness
Tendency to put the blame regarding own problems on others
Rejects letting go of the past and limiting belief systems
Hand positions: first and fourth chakras
Deletion: judge program, love hurts program, unable to forgive program
Archangels: Haniel,Sandalphon, Jophiel, Raphael, Jeremiel, Zadkiel, Chamuel

Enteritis
Programs and emotions:
Indecisive
Can't relax
Suppressed hatred
Hand positions: first and second chakras
Deletion: love hurts program
Archangels: Raphael, Chamuel

Epilepsy
Programs and emotions:
Feels chased
Has a need to punish her/himself
Sees life as a battle
Hand positions: fourth, sixth, and seventh chakras
Deletion: victim program
Archangels: Chamuel, Raziel, Metatron

Exhaustion, chronic

Programs and emotions:
Is desperate
Feels misunderstood
Feels left alone
Feels hopeless
Is tired of life's struggles
Lacks self-confidence
Hand positions: fourth chakra
Deletion: victim program
Archangels: Raphael, Chamuel

Eye problems

Programs and emotions:
Can't see and accept reality
Can't forgive
Fears unpleasant news and decisions
Fears the future (myopic)
Fears the present (hyperopic)
Rage and disappointment (conjunctivitis)
With children: doesn't want to see what is happening in the family

cataracts

Programs and emotions:
Does not want to look into the future
Can't accept future events
Feels threatened
Hand positions: sixth chakra
Deletion: victim program
Archangels: Raziel, Chamuel

conjunctivitis
Programs and emotions:
Feels that she/he does not do the right thing
Is furious about others
Can't forgive
Hand positions: sixth chakra
Deletion: unable to forgive program
Archangels: Raziel, Jeremiel, Zadkiel

glaucoma
Programs and emotions:
Can't forgive
Deep pain and emotional wounds
Feels under pressure
Hand positions: sixth chakra
Deletion: unable to forgive program
Archangels: Raziel, Jeremiel, Zadkiel

rings below the eyes
Programs and emotions:
Feels as though others do not understand her/him
Feels unfulfilled
Resentment
Emotional injuries due to rejection
Deeply rooted mourning and regret
Self reproaches, she/he blames her/himself
Hand positions: sixth chakra
Deletion: unable to forgive program
Archangels: Azrael, Raziel, Jeremiel, Zadkiel

squinting
Programs and emotions:
Fears to hear the truth
Fear of punishment
Doesn't want to see what happens
Hand positions: sixth chakra
Deletion: victim program
Archangels: Raziel, Chamuel

sty
Programs and emotions:
Anger at her/himself and others
Can't forgive
Is hostile
Hand positions: sixth chakra
Deletion: unable to forgive program
Archangels: Raziel, Jeremiel, Zadkiel

swollen eyes
Programs and emotions:
Can't let go
Rigid and set opinions
Hand positions: fourth chakra
Deletion: victim program, unable to forgive program
Archangels: Chamuel, Jeremiel, Zadkiel

twitching
Programs and emotions:
Fears not having enough time
Can't stand unfinished business
Weak, when having to make decisions
Hand positions: sixth chakra
Deletion: victim program
Archangels: Raziel, Chamuel

Facial problems, general

Programs and emotions:
Feels rejected
Self-doubt
Relationship problems
Hand positions: second and fourth chakras
Deletion: love hurts program
Archangels: Raphael, Chamuel, Gabriel

facial paralysis

Programs and emotions:
Self-condemnation
Hand positions: second and fourth chakras
Deletion: judge program
Archangels: Raphael, Chamuel, Gabriel, Jophiel

Fainting

Programs and emotions:
Feels crushed by his/her own current life situation
Hopelessness
Fears current happenings
Fears future happenings
Hand positions: first, third, and sixth chakras
Deletion: victim program
Archangels: Sandalphon, Michael, Raphael, Uriel, Raziel

Fear

Programs and emotions:
Feels unable to change a situation
Feels helpless and weak
No confidence
Hand positions: all chakras
Deletion: victim program

Archangels: Raphael, Michael, Gabriel, Uriel, Raziel, Metatron, Chamuel

Feet, problems with
Programs and emotions:
Does not accept his/her own way of life
Left: the spiritual life
Right: the physical and material aspect of life
Fears the future
Is afraid to make the next step
Lacks understanding of him/herself and others
Hand positions: fourth chakra
Deletion: unable to forgive program
Archangels: Chamuel, Jeremiel, Zadkiel

Fibroids
Programs and emotions:
Feels hurt by the partner
Can't forgive
Feels attacked in her femininity
Feelings of revenge
Hand positions: second and fourth chakras
Deletion: love hurts program, unable to forgive program, judge program
Archangels: Haniel, Raphael, Chamuel, Zadkiel, Jophiel, Jeremiel, Gabriel

Fistula
Programs and emotions:
Can't let go
Feels powerless and helpless
Can't forgive
Hand positions: fourth chakra

Deletion: unable to forgive program, victim program
Archangels: Chamuel, Jeremiel, Zadkiel

Frigidity
Programs and emotions:
Fear and guilt regarding sexuality
Can't accept
Refusal of own femininity
Limiting belief pattern (e.g., "sex is bad")
Hand positions: second and fourth chakras
Deletion: unable to forgive program
Archangels: Haniel, Gabriel, Raphael, Chamuel, Jeremiel, Zadkiel

Fungal infections
Programs and emotions:
Feels weak
Feels exhausted
Can't let go of the past
Can't accept the present
Can't forgive
Hand positions: second, third, fourth, and sixth chakras
Deletion: love hurts program
Archangels: Raphael, Chamuel, Gabriel, Raziel

Gallbladder
Programs and emotions:
Feels bitterness
Too proud to forgive
Wants to force things
Hand positions: third chakra
Deletion: unable to forgive program
Archangels: Michael, Raphael, Uriel, Jeremiel, Zadkiel

gallstones

Programs and emotions:
Suppressed and not released bitterness
Too proud to forgive
Feels helpless in current life situation
Feels dependent on others
Feels unprotected
Hand positions: third chakra
Deletion: victim program, unable to forgive program
Archangels: Michael, Raphael, Chamuel, Uriel, Jeremiel, Zadkiel

Giddiness

Programs and emotions:
Lack of balance
Feels confused, not focused
Feels overburdened
The sense of life is not clear
Rejects the current life situation
The ego suppresses the search for spirituality
Conflict between emotions and thoughts
Hand positions: fourth, fifth, sixth, and seventh chakras
Deletion: love hurts program
Archangels: Chamuel, Raphael, Zadkiel, Raziel, Metatron

Glandular problems

Programs and emotions:
No contact to own God power
Lives in the past
Feels inhibited
Doesn't dare to be active
Lacks self-confidence
Is not balanced

Hand positions: fifth, sixth, and seventh chakras
Deletion: victim program
Archangels: Michael, Raphael, Chamuel, Zadkiel, Raziel, Metatron

Graying hair
Programs and emotions:
Lacks self-love
Lacks self-confidence
Feels not good enough
Is stressed
Overnight: shock
Hand positions: fourth chakra
Deletion: love hurts program
Archangels: Raphael, Chamuel

Hair loss
Programs and emotions:
Doesn't feel appreciated
Feels as though others do not understand him/her
Feels insecure
Relies rather on him/herself than on others
Is not in the his/her own power
Hand positions: second and fourth chakras
Deletion: love hurts program
Archangels: Raphael, Chamuel, Gabriel

Halitosis
Programs and emotions:
Feels unloved
Feels treated unjustly
Can't forgive
Can't let go of old memories

Hand positions: fourth and fifth chakras
Deletion: unable to forgive program, victim program
Archangels: Raphael, Chamuel, Zadkiel, Jeremiel

Hay fever
Programs and emotions:
Suppressed fear
Suppressed rage
Suppressed grief
Suppressed tears
Lacks self-love
Hand positions: fourth, sixth, and seventh chakras
Deletion: love hurts program, victim program
Archangels: Azrael, Raphael, Chamuel, Raziel, Metatron

Headache
Programs and emotions:
Is tense and stressed
Feels under pressure
Fears being unable to fulfill the expectations of others
(also those of his/her parents)
Self-criticism
Lacks self- love
Unsatisfactory relationships
Suppressed emotional pain
Can't let go
Hand positions: fourth, sixth, and seventh chakras
Deletion: love hurts program, unable to forgive program,
victim program
Archangels: Raphael, Raziel, Metatron, Chamuel, Jere-
miel, Zadkiel

Heart problems
Programs and emotions:
Feels overburdened and stressed
Sees no way out of the current situation
Feels unloved
Feels not supported by others
Feels no joy
Feels too much pressure on him/herself and has too much responsibility
Can't forgive her/himself and others
Lives an unhappy relationship
Hand positions: first and second chakras
Deletion: love hurts program
Archangels: Sandalphon, Raphael, Chamuel, Jeremiel, Zadkiel

Heartburn
Programs and emotions:
Feels unfree
Great fear
Suppressed emotions:
Doesn't have his/her life under control
Hand positions: first, third, fourth, and fifth chakras
Deletion: victim program, love hurts program
Archangels: Sandalphon, Michael, Raphael, Uriel, Chamuel, Zadkiel

Hepatitis
Programs and emotions:
Fear, anger, hate
Can't forgive
Fears and rejects change
Hand positions: third, fourth, and fifth chakras

Deletion: unable to forgive program
Archangels: Jeremiel, Zadkiel, Chamuel, Michael, Raphael, Uriel

Hip problems
Programs and emotions:
Is scared to go forward
Has problems making important decisions
Does not feel supported
Has problems accepting current experiences
Hand positions: first, second, and third chakras
Deletion: victim program
Archangels: Raphael, Chamuel, Gabriel

Hyperactivity
Programs and emotions:
Feels frustrated
Feels helpless
Feels inner agitation
Furious with parents (children)
Hand positions: fourth chakra
Deletion: victim program
Archangels: Chamuel

Immune deficiency
Programs and emotions:
Feels overburdened
Feels unfree, controlled, and suppressed
Fears losing someone or something
Feels abandoned
Feels defenseless and unprotected
Hand positions: fourth chakra
Deletion: victim program
Archangels: Chamuel

Immune system, disturbances of
Programs and emotions:
No inner balance
No inner peace
Wants to give up
No empathy for others
Loss of control
Doesn't feel good enough
Hand positions: all chakras
Deletion: victim program
Archangels: Raphael, Michael, Gabriel, Uriel

Impotence
Programs and emotions:
Fears and feels guilt regarding sexuality
Feels rejected
Suppressed conflicts with mother
Suppressed frustrations coming from former partners/ relationships
Complexes regarding fear of failing/being a failure
Hand positions: first, second, fourth, and fifth chakras
Deletion: love hurts program
Archangels: Sandalphon, Raphael, Chamuel, Gabriel, Zadkiel

Incontinence
Programs and emotions:
Abundance of suppressed emotions
Feels guilt toward her/himself
Fear of failure
Hand positions: second and fourth chakras
Deletion: love hurts program, judge program
Archangels: Raphael, Jophiel, Gabriel

Infections
Programs and emotions:
Hostile feelings toward others
Anger and rage
Can't forgive
Can't trust others
Hand positions: fourth chakra
Deletion: unable to forgive program
Archangels: Jeremiel, Chamuel, Zadkiel

Inflammation of the vocal chords
Programs and emotions:
Feels overburdened
Feels speechless, helpless
Feels abandoned
Hand positions: fifth chakra
Deletion: victim program
Archangels: Chamuel, Zadkiel

Influenza
Programs and emotions:
Is scared of future events
Fears social crisis
Fears economical crisis
Fears catastrophes/disasters
Negative belief systems and pattern, accepted from society
Hand positions: second and fourth chakras
Deletion: love hurts program, unable to forgive program,
victim program
Archangels: Raphael, Chamuel, Gabriel, Jeremiel, Zadkiel

Insomnia
Programs and emotions:
Feels insecure
Feels stressed
Feels guilty
Fears punishment
Fears changes
Can't let go
Can't forgive him/herself and others
Hand positions: fourth, fifth, and sixth chakras
Deletion: unable to forgive program
Archangels: Chamuel, Jeremiel, Zadkiel, Raziel

Intestinal diseases
Programs and emotions:
Needs love, affection, and attention
Feels down and beaten
Is worried all the time
Hand positions: first and second chakras
Deletion: victim program, love hurts program
Archangels: Chamuel, Sandalphon, Gabriel, Raphael

Jaw problems
Programs and emotions:
Can't forgive
Can't handle the past
Anger and rage
Feeling of revenge
Hand positions: fourth and fifth chakras
Deletion: unable to forgive program
Archangels: Jeremiel, Chamuel, Zadkiel

Joint problems
Programs and emotions:
Rejects changes
Lacks flexibility
Suppressed emotional pain
Hand positions: fourth and fifth chakras
Deletion: love hurts program
Archangels: Raphael, Chamuel

Kidney stones
Programs and emotions:
Suppressed rage
Hand positions: first, second, and fourth chakras
Deletion: judge program, love hurts program
Archangels: Sandalphon, Chamuel, Raphael, Gabriel, Jophiel

Kidney weakness
Programs and emotions:
Feels unloved
Feels guilty
Feels helpless
Fears criticism
Disharmony in relationship
Hand positions: first, second, and fourth chakras
Deletion: victim program, love hurts program
Archangels: Sandalphon, Chamuel, Raphael, Gabriel

Knee problems
Programs and emotions:
Feels inflexible
Rejects change, stubbornness
Accumulated anger and aggression

Can't admit own mistakes (pride)
Fears future
Left side: feels insecure
Is stressed
Can't accept certain events
Right hand side: feels the need to assert own position, rigidity
Encounters resistance when asserting own interests and needs
Rejects authority
Hand positions: fourth and fifth chakras
Deletion: unable to forgive program
Archangels: Jeremiel, Zadkiel, Chamuel

Laryngitis
Programs and emotions:
Suppressed rage and anger
Feels treated unjustly
Fears to express own needs
Hand positions: fifth chakra
Deletion: victim program
Archangels: Chamuel, Zadkiel

Left side of body, problems on
Programs and emotions:
Suppressed emotion towards women (mother)
Rejects own femininity
Longing for spirituality
Can't forgive
Can't accept
Hand positions: fourth, fifth, and sixth chakras
Deletion: unable to forgive program
Archangels: Haniel, Raziel, Jeremiel, Zadkiel, Chamuel

Legs, disturbed energy flow in
Programs and emotions:
Fears the future
Fears changes
Feels financially insecure
Hand positions: first and third chakras
Deletion: victim program
Archangels: Chamuel, Sandalphon, Michael, Raphael, Uriel

Liver diseases
Programs and emotions:
Rage, anger, hate
Can't let go the past
Can't forgive
Is possessive and dogmatic
Fears and rejects changes
Hand positions: third, fourth, and fifth chakras
Deletion: judge program, unable to forgive program
Archangels: Chamuel, Jophiel, Jeremiel, Zadkiel, Michael, Uriel

Low energy/drive
Programs and emotions:
Feels as though others don't understand him/her
Feels unloved
Can't let go
Can't forgive
Hand positions: third and fourth chakras
Deletion: unable to forgive program, love hurts program
Archangels: Michael, Raphael, Uriel, Jeremiel, Zadkiel

Lymph blockage
Programs and emotions:
Lacks joy of life
Lacks enthusiasm
Doesn't feel accepted
Doesn't accept him/herself
Limited thought patterns
Hand positions: fourth and fifth chakras
Deletion: victim program, love hurts program
Archangels: Raphael, Chamuel, Zadkiel

Menopausal problems
Programs and emotions:
Feels useless
Does not feel well balanced
Is angry at her/himself
Self-refusal
Fears getting old
Hand positions: fourth chakra
Deletion: judge program, love hurts program
Archangels: Chamuel, Raphael, Zadkiel

Migraine
Programs and emotions:
Feels under pressure
Loss of control
Feels sexually not balanced
Opposition against own sense of responsibility
Opposition against duties (family, work)
Can't let go
Hand positions: fourth, sixth and seventh chakras
Deletion: love hurts program
Archangels: Raphael, Raziel, Metatron, Chamuel

Miscarriage
Programs and emotions:
Feels not prepared yet/not ready
Feels that the time for childbirth is wrong
Lack of self-love and acceptance
Fears the future
Fears responsibility
Hand positions: first, second, and fourth chakras
Deletion: victim program
Archangels: Sandalphon, Chamuel

Mouth problems
Programs and emotions:
Feels unloved
Feels threatened
Opposition to change
Fears changes
Hand positions: fourth and fifth chakras
Deletion: love hurts program, victim program
Archangels: Raphael, Chamuel, Zadkiel

Multiple sclerosis
Programs and emotions:
Feels as though others do not understand her/him
Feels guilty
Is hard to her/himself
Can't forgive
Hand positions: sixth chakra
Deletion: judge program, unable to forgive program
Archangels: Raziel, Jeremiel, Zadkiel, Jophiel

Muscle problems/muscle cramps
Programs and emotions:
Feels guilty
Feels like a loser/failure
Fears the future
Rejects new things/news
Hand positions: first, fourth, and fifth chakras
Deletion: victim program
Archangels: Sandalphon, Raphael, Chamuel, Zadkiel

Nail chewing
Programs and emotions:
Frustration
Feels as though others do not understand her/him
Feels unfulfilled
Opposition and defiance against parents
Hand positions: fourth and fifth chakras
Deletion: victim program, love hurts program
Archangels: Chamuel, Raphael, Zadkiel

Nausea
Programs and emotions:
Insecurity
Feels rejected
Lacks trust in the current life situation
Fears failure
Hand positions: third, fourth, fifth, and sixth chakras
Deletion: victim program
Archangels: Michael, Raphael, Uriel, Chamuel, Zadkiel, Raziel

Neck problems
Programs and emotions:
Feels under pressure
Feels immobile
Feels hemmed in/restricted
Opposition against other points of view
Is stubborn
Can't give in
Hand positions: fifth chakra
Deletion: victim program
Archangels: Chamuel, Zadkiel

Nerve problems
Programs and emotions:
Feels crushed down/overwhelmed by current situation
Can't relax, get away from it all
Can't resist/defend him/herself
Can't talk about own needs
Can't let go of the past
Thoughts and emotions are contrary
Hand positions: third chakra
Deletion: victim program
Archangels: Michael, Raphael, Uriel, Chamuel

Nervousness
Programs and emotions:
Is scared by the future
Is irritated/confused
Can't talk about own needs
Lacks trust in her/himself and others
Hand positions: third and sixth chakras
Deletion: victim program
Archangels: Michael, Raphael, Uriel, Chamuel, Raziel

Neuralgia
Programs and emotions:
Feelings of Guilt
Feels rightfully punished
Can't forgive her/himself
Hand positions: fourth and sixth chakras
Deletion: victim program, unable to forgive program
Archangels: Jeremiel, Zadkiel, Chamuel, Raziel

Nose polyps
Programs and emotions:
Feels unloved
Has no joy in life/takes no pleasure in it
Feels under pressure
Hand positions: fourth chakra
Deletion: victim program
Archangels: Chamuel, Raphael

Nose polyps in children
Programs and emotions:
Feels stress, tension and conflicts within the family
Feels unloved
Feels unwelcome
Feels as though she/he is in her/his parents way
Hand positions: fourth chakra
Deletion: of unwanted emotions/see list page xx
Archangels: Chamuel, Raphael, Metatron

Nose, runny
Programs and emotions:
Feels helpless
Feels left alone/abandoned
Feels as though others don't consider him/her

Doesn't want to take responsibility
Hand positions: fourth and fifth chakras
Deletion: love hurts program
Archangels: Chamuel, Raphael, Zadkiel

Nosebleed
Programs and emotions:
Feels unloved
Feels ignored
Feels worthless
Hand positions: fourth chakra
Deletion: victim program
Archangel: Chamuel

Numbness
Programs and emotions:
Feels rejected
Feels unimportant
Difficulty in expressing her/himself
Lack of self-love
Hand positions: fifth and sixth chakras
Deletion: love hurts program, victim program
Archangels: Raphael, Chamuel, Zadkiel, Raziel

Obesity
Programs and emotions:
Feels defenseless
Feels insecure
Feels vulnerable
Lacks self-love
Hand positions: third, fourth, fifth, and sixth chakras
Deletion: victim program, love hurts program
Archangels: Michael, Raphael, Uriel, Chamuel, Zadkiel, Raziel

Osteoporosis
Programs and emotions:
Feels under pressure
Mental stress
Lack of support in life
Hand positions: fourth and fifth chakras
Deletion: victim program
Archangels: Chamuel, Zadkiel

Ovaries, problems with
Programs and emotions:
Feels lonely and abandoned
Suppressed creativity
Need for love and respect
Feels sexually incapable
Hand positions: first and second chakras
Deletion: victim program
Archangels: Haniel, Raphael, Chamuel

Pain
Programs and emotions:
Feels guilt
Self-punishment
Feels unhappy in relationships
Lacks self-love
Hand positions: all chakras
Deletion: All programs: love hurts program, victim program, unable to forgive program, judge program
Archangels: Sandalphon, Michael, Raphael, Uriel, Chamuel, Jeremiel, Zadkiel, Metatron, Raziel, Gabriel

Pain in the arm, left
Programs and emotions:
Can't accept
Can't accept own femininity
Emotions toward women (mother and others), not yet released, not processed
Connection to own spirituality is not strong enough
Hand positions: fourth and fifth chakras
Deletion: love hurts program
Archangels: Michael, Haniel, Raziel, Chamuel, Raphael

Pain in the arm, right
Programs and emotions:
Can't give
Can't let go
Has difficulty in accepting reality
Can't accept own masculinity
Unprocessed emotions toward males (father and so on)
Insufficient connection to own body
Hand positions: fourth and fifth chakras
Deletion: unable to forgive program
Archangels: Chamuel, Jeremiel, Zadkiel

Pancreatitis
Programs and emotions:
Feels unhappy
Feels guilty and ashamed/embarrassed
Feels unloved
Can't allow joy and laughter
Suppressed anger
Fears new things/events
Hand positions: first, third, fourth, and fifth chakras
Deletion: judge program, love hurts program

Archangels: Sandalphon, Michael, Raphael, Uriel, Chamuel, Zadkiel, Jophiel

Paralysis
Programs and emotions:
Feels trapped in the current life situation
Feels crushed by responsibility
Fears the future
Hand positions: fourth, fifth, and sixth chakras
Deletion: victim program
Archangels: Chamuel, Jophiel, Jeremiel, Zadkiel, Raziel

Parkinson's disease
Programs and emotions:
Great fear without being aware of what one actually fears
Need to control things
Lacks feeling of self worth/respect
Lacks self-love
Lacks trust in her/himself and others
(Please also check toxic load of mercury in blood)
Hand positions: all chakras
Deletion: victim program, love hurts program
Archangels: Sandalphon, Michael, Raphael, Uriel, Chamuel, Jeremiel, Zadkiel, Metatron, Raziel, Gabriel

Phlebitis
Programs and emotions:
Frustration
Tendency to blame others
Suppressed fury
Lacks joy in life, takes no pleasure in life
Hand positions: first, second, fourth, and fifth chakras
Deletion: judge program

Archangels: Sandalphon, Gabriel, Chamuel, Zadkiel, Raphael, Jophiel

Phobias
Programs and emotions:
Feels defenseless
Unprotected
Vulnerable
Hand positions: all chakras
Deletion: victim program, love hurts program, unable to forgive program
Archangels: Sandalphon, Michael, Raphael, Uriel, Azrael, Chamuel, Jeremiel, Zadkiel, Metatron, Raziel, Gabriel

Phobias are deeply rooted fears of:
illness, darkness, flight travels, driving by car, heights, bridges, tunnels, elevators, escalators, graveyards, fire, water, insects, spiders, aggressions from/by animals, public places, public performances, crowds.
The fear of: hearing voices, being abandoned, being controlled, being punished, being abused, having to die, etc.

Pimples
Programs and emotions:
Frustration
Fear to get hurt
Suppressed rage and anger
Hand positions: second, fourth, and fifth chakras
Deletion: love hurts program
Archangels: Raphael, Chamuel, Gabriel

Pneumonia
Programs and emotions:
Is desperate

Doesn't feel supported
Lack of self-love
Hand positions: fourth and fifth chakras
Deletion: love hurts program, victim program
Archangels: Raphael, Chamuel, Zadkiel

Premenstrual tension
Programs and emotions:
Feels powerless
Feels weak
Feels not balanced
Feels vulnerable
Feels as though she is controlled by others (hormones)
Can't help this, can't defend
Rejects this part of femininity
Lacks self-love
Hand positions: first and fourth chakras
Deletion: victim program, love hurts program, unable to forgive program
Archangels: Haniel, Sandalphon, Jophiel, Raphael, Jeremiel, Zadkiel

Prostate problems
Programs and emotions:
Fears loss of control
Fears rejection
Fears getting old
Sexual pressure, guilt feelings
Can't let go of the past
Can't forgive
Hand positions: first and second chakras
Deletion: unable to forgive program
Archangels: Jeremiel, Zadkiel, Sandalphon, Gabriel, Raphael

Pulmonary disease
Programs and emotions:
Doesn't feel worth of living healthy
Grief
Lack of appreciation in life
Monotony in life
Hand positions: fourth and fifth chakras
Deletion: love hurts program, victim program
Archangels: Azrael, Raphael, Chamuel, Zadkiel

Pyelitis
Programs and emotions:
Feels unloved
Is disappointed and furious
Disharmony in relationship
Feels that the partner doesn't understand her/him regarding sexuality
Neglect of own needs
Fear to fail
Existential fears
Hand positions: first, second, and fourth chakras
Deletion: victim program, love hurts program
Archangels: Sandalphon, Chamuel, Raphael, Gabriel

Rash
Programs and emotions:
Feels conflicts in current life situation (within the family)
Feels frustrated because she/he is unsuccessful in reaching aims
Feels insecure
Hand positions: second, fourth, and fifth chakras
Deletion: love hurts program
Archangels: Raphael, Chamuel, Gabriel

Rheumatoid arthritis
Programs and emotions:
Feels as others do not understand him/her
Feels punished and rejected by others
Lacks self love
Hand positions: second, fourth, and fifth chakras
Deletion: victim program, love hurts program
Archangels: Gabriel, Chamuel, Raphael, Zadkiel

Right side of body, problems with
Programs and emotions:
Can't forgive
Can't share
Suppressed emotions towards men (father)
Rejection of own masculinity
Fears responsibility
Wish for security and matter
Hand positions: first, second, third, and fourth chakras
Deletion: unable to forgive program
Archangels: Sandalphon, Raphael, Chamuel, Gabriel, Jeremiel, Zadkiel

Sciatica
Programs and emotions:
Fears of not being able to live out own creativity
Suppressed needs
Sexual frustration
Lies to her/himself and others
Fears lack of money
Hand positions: first, second, and third chakras
Deletion: love hurts program, victim program
Archangels: Sandalphon, Raphael, Chamuel, Gabriel, Michael, Uriel

Shingles
Programs and emotions:
Feels insecure
Is stressed and tense
Can't let go
Doesn't want to take responsibility
Deep emotional sorrow
Hand positions: fourth and fifth chakras
Deletion: unable to forgive program, victim program
Archangels: Chamuel, Zadkiel

Shoulder problems
Programs and emotions:
Feels guilty
Lacks joy of life
Feels discouraged and hopeless
Feels burdened and tension
Feels indispensable
Takes over too much responsibility
Hand positions: fourth and fifth chakras
Deletion: victim program, love hurts program
Archangels: Chamuel, Raphael, Zadkiel

Sinusitis
Programs and emotions:
Feels irritated by a related person
Feels under pressure
Suppressed rage
Hand positions: fourth and sixth chakras
Deletion: victim program
Archangels: Chamuel, Raphael, Raziel

Skin diseases

Programs and emotions:
Is restless
Bored
Feels insecure
Feels threatened
Suppressed criticism
Suppressed irritation
Limiting belief systems
Hand positions: second, fourth, and fifth chakras
Deletion: love hurts program, victim program
Archangels: Raphael, Chamuel, Gabriel

Slipped disc

Programs and emotions:
Feels abandoned
Has too much responsibility
Painful separation (past or present)
Hand positions: second chakra
Deletion: victim program
Archangels: Gabriel, Chamuel, Raphael

Snoring

Programs and emotions:
Refusal of further development
Refusal to let go of old programs
Rejects change
Lacks self-love
Hand positions: fourth and fifth chakras
Deletion: love hurts program, unable to forgive program
Archangels: Chamuel, Raphael, Jeremiel, Zadkiel

Sore throat
Programs and emotions:
Can't forgive him/herself and others
Feels restricted/confined
Has difficulties expressing own needs
Suppressed anger and fury
Suppressed emotional injuries
Hand positions: fourth and fifth chakras
Deletion: love hurts program, unable to forgive program
Archangels: Raphael, Chamuel, Zadkiel, Jeremiel

Spinal problems
Programs and emotions:
Feels inferior
Lacks support in life
Can't let go
Can't accept
Mentally and ego-controlled
Fear of living emotions:
Hand positions: fifth chakras
Deletion: victim program
Archangels: Chamuel, Zadkiel, Raphael

Cervical vertebrae, slipped
C1
Programs and emotions:
Feels that others don't understand her/him
Feels unbalanced
Feels not good enough
Fears punishment
Hand positions: fifth chakra
Deletion: victim program
Archangels: Chamuel, Zadkiel

C2

Programs and emotions:
Indecision
Conflict between emotions and thoughts
Opposition to oneself
Rejection of spirituality
Hand positions: fifth chakra
Deletion: judge program
Archangels: Chamuel, Jophiel

C3

Programs and emotions:
Guilt feelings
Indecision
Lacks self-love
Hand positions: fifth chakra
Deletion: victim program
Archangels: Chamuel, Zadkiel

C4

Programs and emotions:
Feels guilty
Feels bitter
Can't forgive
Can't let go of the past
Hand positions: fifth chakra
Deletion: unable to forgive program
Archangels: Chamuel, Jeremiel, Zadkiel

C5

Programs and emotions:
Feels rejected
Feels overburdened

Can't accept
Fears rejection
Fears humiliation
Hand positions: fifth chakra
Deletion: victim program
Archangels: Chamuel, Zadkiel

C6
Programs and emotions:
Feels unloved
Doesn't feel lovable
Feels overburdened
Feels the need to change others
Hand positions: fifth chakra
Deletion: love hurts program
Archangels: Chamuel, Zadkiel, Raphael

C7
Programs and emotions:
Helplessness
Lack of support
Can't forgive
Can't let go
Hand positions: fifth chakra
Deletion: love hurts program, unable to forgive program
Archangels: Chamuel, Zadkiel, Raphael, Jeremiel

Thoracic vertebrae, slipped
T1
Programs and emotions:
Feels overstrained
Fears failure
Fears life
Hand positions: fourth chakra

Deletion: victim program
Archangel: Chamuel

T2
Programs and emotions:
Feels hurt
Feels abandoned
Lacks self-love
Hand positions: fourth chakra
Deletion: victim program, love hurts program
Archangels: Chamuel, Raphael

T3
Programs and emotions:
Feels hurt
Feels guilty
Can't forgive
Hand positions: fourth chakra
Deletion: victim program, unable to forgive program
Archangels: Chamuel, Jeremiel, Zadkiel

T4
Programs and emotions:
Feels bitterness
Feels guilty
Can't forgive
Hand positions: fourth chakra
Deletion: unable to forgive program
Archangels: Chamuel, Jeremiel, Zadkiel

T5
Programs and emotions:
Feels treated unjustly
Can't forgive

Accumulated rage
Hand positions: fourth chakra
Deletion: unable to forgive program
Archangels: Chamuel, Jeremiel, Zadkiel

T6

Programs and emotions:
Fears the future
Can't trust
Can't forgive
Accumulated rage
Hand positions: fourth chakra
Deletion: unable to forgive program
Archangels: Chamuel, Jeremiel, Zadkiel

T7

Programs and emotions:
Feels hurt
Feels bitterness
Can't let go
Can't forgive
Hand positions: fourth chakra
Deletion: unable to forgive program
Archangels: Chamuel, Jeremiel, Zadkiel

T8

Programs and emotions:
Feels unloved
Feels as though she/he has failed
Lacks self-love
Hand positions: fourth chakra
Deletion: victim program
Archangel: Chamuel

T9
Programs and emotions:
Feels unloved
Feels as though others do not understand her/him
Feels abandoned
Hand positions: fourth chakra
Deletion: victim program
Archangels: Chamuel

T10
Programs and emotions:
Feels as though others do not understand her/him
Feels not appreciated
Doesn't want to take the responsibility for her/himself
Hand positions: fourth chakra
Deletion: victim program
Archangels: Chamuel

T11
Programs and emotions:
Doesn't feel lovable
Lacks self-love
Fears relationships
Hand positions: fourth chakra
Deletion: love hurts program
Archangels: Chamuel, Raphael

T12
Programs and emotions:
Lacks joy of life
Depression
Insecurity
Fears relationships
Hand positions: fourth chakra

Deletion: love hurts program
Archangels: Chamuel, Raphael

Lumbar vertebrae, slipped
L1
Programs and emotions:
Feels unloved
Insecurity
Lacks support
Hand positions: third chakra
Deletion: love hurts program
Archangels: Michael, Raphael, Uriel

L2
Programs and emotions:
Deep disappointment
Grief coming from childhood
Hand positions: third chakra
Deletion: love hurts program
Archangels: Michael, Raphael, Uriel

L3
Programs and emotions:
Guilt feelings
Self-hate
Can't let go of past sexual problems
Hand positions: third chakra
Deletion: love hurts program, unable to forgive program
Archangels: Michael, Raphael, Uriel, Jeremiel, Zadkiel

L4
Programs and emotions:
Feels unloved

Feels powerless
Lack of self-esteem
Existential fear
Problems with sexuality
Hand positions: third chakra
Deletion: love hurts program, victim program
Archangels: Michael, Raphael, Uriel, Chamuel

L5
Programs and emotions:
Lacks joy of live
Can't accept joy and lust
Insecurity
Feels as though others do not understand him/her
Hand positions: third chakra
Deletion: love hurts program
Archangels: Michael, Raphael, Uriel

Sacrum
Programs and emotions:
Powerlessness
Insecurity
Accumulated rage
Can't forgive
Hand positions: first chakra
Deletion: unable to forgive program
Archangels: Sandalphon, Jeremiel, Zadkiel

Coccyx
Programs and emotions:
Feels unloved
Feels unbalanced
Can't forgive
Self-punishment

Hand positions: first chakra
Deletion: victim program, unable to forgive program
Archangels: Sandalphon, Jeremiel, Zadkiel

Splenopathy
Programs and emotions:
Feels unloved
Lacks self-love
Intensive anger
Can't let go
Can't forgive
Hand positions: third chakra
Deletion: victim program, unable to forgive program
Archangels: Michael, Raphael, Uriel, Chamuel, Jeremiel, Zadkiel

Sprain
Programs and emotions:
Feels abandoned
Anger
Lack of self-confidence
Rejects current life situation
Hand positions: first and fourth chakras
Deletion: judge program, unable to forgive program
Archangels: Sandalphon, Chamuel, Jeremiel, Zadkiel, Jophiel

Stomach pain
Programs and emotions:
Worries about others, possessive
Feels obliged to always be understanding
Feels insignificant
Suppressed tension
Fears being abandoned

Feels disharmony in relationship
Lacks trust
Hand positions: third chakra
Deletion: love hurts program
Archangels: Michael, Raphael, Uriel

Stomach problems
Programs and emotions:
Feels unhappy
Feels unloved
Feels insecure and existentially threatened
Swallows rage and fear of new things/situations
Hand positions: first, third, fourth, and fifth chakras
Deletion: victim program, love hurts program
Archangels: Sandalphon, Michael, Raphael, Uriel, Chamuel, Zadkiel

Stress, tendency towards
Programs and emotions:
Feels unprotected/defenseless
Lacks support
Feels opposition from others
Hand positions: first, second, third, and fourth chakras
Deletion: victim program
Archangels: Sandalphon, Gabriel, Raphael, Michael, Uriel, Chamuel, Zadkiel

Stroke
Programs and emotions:
Feels under pressure
Is dissatisfied with his/her current life situation
Resistant to change

Self-destructive patterns and behavior
Can't let go (past)
Can't accept (present/future)
Hand positions: first, third, and fourth chakras
Deletion: unable to forgive program
Archangels: Sandalphon, Jeremiel, Zadkiel, Chamuel

Temperature, high
Programs and emotions:
Is angry at others and him/herself
Is irritated by complicated and messy environment
Suppressed emotions are cooking up
Hand positions: fourth chakra
Deletion: unable to forgive program
Archangels: Chamuel, Jeremiel, Zadkiel

Thyroid problems
Programs and emotions:
Feels humiliated
Feels frustrated
Feels unfree
Feels controlled and restricted
Lacks self-love
Unable to express oneself
Lacks creativity
Conflict with emotions and thoughts
Hand positions: fourth and fifth chakras
Deletion: unable to forgive program, victim program
Archangels: Chamuel, Jeremiel, Zadkiel

Tinnitus
Programs and emotions:
Feels overburdened
Feels that others don't understand her/him

Looks for a way out of his/her current life-situation
Searches for spirituality
Hand positions: fourth, fifth, and sixth chakras
Deletion: love hurts program
Archangels: Raphael, Chamuel, Zadkiel, Raziel

Tongue problems
Programs and emotions:
Feels unhappy
Feels guilt
Can't accept good things
Lacks joy of life
Hand positions: fourth and fifth chakras
Deletion: victim program, love hurts program
Archangels: Chamuel, Raphael, Zadkiel

Tonsillitis
Programs and emotions:
Feels that others don't understand her/him
Feels unloved
Suppressed anger and rage
Unable to talk about own feelings
Hand positions: fourth and fifth chakras
Deletion: love hurts program, victim program
Archangels: Raphael, Chamuel, Zadkiel

Travel sickness
Programs and emotions:
Feels controlled/directed by others
Fears loss of control
Can't let go
Hand positions: third and fourth chakras
Deletion: victim program
Archangels: Michael, Raphael, Uriel, Chamuel

Tuberculosis
Programs and emotions:
Rage and aggression
Jealousy
Feels the need to punish others
Tendency to take possession of everything
Lacks self-love
Hand positions: fourth, fifth, and sixth chakras
Deletion: love hurts program, judge program
Archangels: Raphael, Chamuel, Zadkiel, Raziel, Jophiel

Unconsciousness
Programs and emotions:
Fears the actual situation
Feels unable to deal with the situation
Is scared of future events
Feels helpless
Refusal to deal with situations
Refusal of further development
Hand positions: first chakra
Deletion: love hurts program
Archangels: Raphael, Sandalphon, Chamuel

Urinary infections
Programs and emotions:
Suppressed rage and anger
Can't forgive
Can't let go
Hand positions: second and fourth chakras
Deletion: unable to forgive program
Archangels: Raphael, Chamuel, Gabriel, Jeremiel, Zadkiel

Uterus, problems with
Programs and emotions:
Suppressed conflicts with mother
Suppressed creativity
Hand positions: first chakra
Deletion: victim program
Archangels: Sandalphon

Varicose veins
Programs and emotions:
Feels under pressure
Feels overburdened
Resistance to heavy pressure of work
Feels discouraged
Would prefer to run away
Hand positions: fourth, fifth, and sixth chakras
Deletion: victim program
Archangels: Raphael, Chamuel, Raziel, Zadkiel

Vomiting
Programs and emotions:
Fears new things/situations/events
Refusal of change
Lacks of self-confidence
Hand positions: third and fourth chakras
Deletion: victim program
Archangels: Michael, Raphael, Uriel, Chamuel

Weight gain
Programs and emotions:
Feels insecure
Feels rejected and abandoned
Feels the need to protect the physical body
Hand positions: second and fourth chakras
Deletion: victim program
Archangels: Gabriel, Raphael, Chamuel

Weight loss (unintentional)
Programs and emotions:
Exaggerated problem with and fear of dangerous situations
Can't trust
Feels extremely tense
Hand positions: first and fourth chakras
Deletion: unable to forgive program
Archangel: Chamuel

Code of Ethics for Quantum Angel Healing Practitioners

1. People come to you with problems they can't resolve alone. Even if your clients claim they are coming to have a treatment "just for fun," you can be sure that deep sorrow and pain are behind their problems. Therefore, you should always take your work seriously and immediately find out what's going on with your client internally. It is your responsibility to encourage and lead your clients with love and respect. Never influence, mislead, or raise false hopes for them.

2. Never work without being asked to, or without the actual permission of your client. Respect the personal needs and privacy of everyone.

3. It is your goal to support and guide people on their spiritual path. Support them by helping them find their inner strength and their own power; however, be aware that you are not there for your client's salvation.

4. Make an appointment with your client, but wait a minimum of three days before you see him or her. This will help the client prepare for the session, and give him or her time to think about any potential questions. Ask your client whether it is all right for the angels to start their work immediately, in preparation for your session. This way, it becomes clearer to your client why he or she needs or wants the treatment. The angels will help your client be open to self-love and self-healing.

5. Please do not schedule emergency appointments! If clients ask you for a last-minute appointment, they often expect you to solve or change a situation, or to see something which isn't there. Often, they would like you to take over the responsibility for their current situation and to make decisions for them, or even tell them what they would like to hear.

6. Please don't be tempted to make your client dependent on you by making appointments for them again and again. This would be an abuse of your power and would only weaken your client. It is tempting to feel needed. Beware! Your ego might open the way for negative energies and trouble. Never think that people need you or your treatment. You would be quite wrong!

7. Quantum Angel Healing practitioners work as clear energy channels and are bound to observe professional confidentiality. All information you get during a healing session has to be held in confidence.

BIBLIOGRAPHY

Benor, Daniel J. *Healing Research. Holistic Energy Medicine and Spirituality.* Munich: Helix Editions Ltd., 1992.

Berger, Peter L. *Auf den Spuren der Engel. Die moderne Gesellschaft und die Wiederentdeckung der Transzendenz.* Freiburg: Herder, 2001.

Borysenko, Joan, and Miroslav Borysenko. *The Power of the Mind to Heal.* Santa Monica, CA: Hay House, 1995.

Braden, Gregg. *The God Code.* Carlsbad, CA: Hay House, 2005.

Bunson, Matthew. *Angels A to Z: A Who's Who of the Heavenly Host.* New York: Three Rivers Press, 1996.

Chopra, Deepak. *Perfect Health.* New York: Three Rivers Press, 1990.

————. *Quantum Healing.* New York: Bantam Books, 1990.

Davies, Philip R., George J. Brooke, and Phillip R. Callaway. *The Complete World of the Dead Sea Scrolls. London, UK:Thames and Hudson, 2002.*

Dieckmann, Dorothea. *Wie Engel erscheinen*. Hamburg: Rotbuch, 2001.

Dossey, Larry. *Be Careful What You Pray For...You Might Just Get It*. San Francisco: HarperSanFrancisco, 1997.

———. *Healing Words*. San Francisco: HarperSanFrancisco, 1997.

Emoto, Masaru. *The Hidden Messages in Water*. New York: Atria, 2005.

Fiore, Edith. *Besessenheit und Heilung, die Befreiung der Seele*. Güllesheim: Silberschnur, 1997.

Gordon, Richard. *Quantum-Touch: The Power to Heal*. Berkeley, CA: North Atlantic Books, 2006.

Hay, Louise. *Heal Your Body*. Santa Monica, CA: Hay House, 1984.

Lewis, James R., and Evelyn Dorothy Oliver. *Angels A to Z*. Detroit: Visible Ink Press, 1996.

Lipton, Bruce, and Steve Bhaerman. *Spontaneous Evolution*. Carlsbad, CA: Hay House, 2009.

MacLean, Dorothy. *Du kannst mit Engeln sprechen*. Munich: Heyne, 1999.

Melody. *Das Handbuch der Edelsteine und Kristalle*. Munich: Droemer Knaur, 2001.

Mohr, Bärbel. *Bestellungen beim Universum*. Aachen: Omega, 1998.

Pert, Candace B. *Molecules of Emotion: The Science Behind Mind-Body Medicine.* New York: Simon & Schuster, 1999.

Ronner, John. *Know Your Angel.* Murfreesboro, TN: Mamre Press, 1993.

Savedow, Steve, ed., trans. *Sepher Razial Hemelach: The Book of the Angel Raziel.* York Beach, ME: Weiser, 2000.

Schroeder, Hans-Werner. *Mensch und Engel. Die Wirklichkeit der Hierarchien.* Frankfurt: Fischer Taschenbuch, 1990.

Spindrift Research. www.spindriftresearch.org.

Verny, Thomas, and John Kelly. *The Secret Life of the Unborn Child.* New York: Dell Publishing, 1988.

Virtue, Doreen. *Angel Medicine.* Carlsbad, CA: Hay House, 2004.

———. *Healing with the Angels.* Santa Monica, CA: Hay House, 1999.

———. *Messages from Your Angels.* Carlsbad, CA: Hay House, 2002.

ABOUT THE AUTHOR

Eva-Maria Mora, a German-born U.S. citizen, overcame a severe illness and underwent amazing life changes which led her to discover a new healing method: Quantum Angel Healing (QAH). When her baby boy was six months old, the doctors told her that she only had a few weeks to live. After this shocking diagnosis, she prayed for help and guidance. Her prayers were answered. She had an encounter with a beautiful angel which changed her life forever. She started to communicate with angels on a regular basis, and they helped her to understand why people get sick, how they can heal themselves, and how they can find their true life purpose. In 2000, Eva-Maria, who has an MBA, was guided to quit her international career as a top management consultant and to let go of everything and everyone in her life. With only two suitcases and a lot of trust, faith, and love in her heart, she came to the United States as an immigrant, not knowing if she would be able to stay in the country. Years of poverty, unemployment, hardship, and painful experiences followed. She understood that all these life lessons were spiritual initiations, which prepared her for her true calling.

Today she is a compassionate, clairvoyant medical intuitive and spiritual teacher. She was approached by

Random House to write a book about her life-changing healing method, QAH. It became a bestseller in Europe, and many more books and CDs about spiritual relationships, children of the light, and how to activate your divine power followed. Together with her husband, Michael, Eva-Maria teaches seminars and QAH certification programs worldwide. She dedicates a lot of her time to charity, helping the new children of the light. She was guided to found a nonprofit organization (www.lichtkinder-lkk.de) and organize the first Children of the Light Conference in Germany in 2010 (www.lichtkinderkonferenz.de). For more information about Eva-Maria and QAH, please visit her web site, www.quantumangel.com, and her blog, www. quantumangelblog.com.

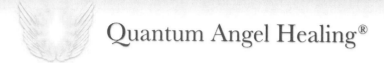
Quantum Angel Healing®

CERTIFICATION PROGRAM

Quantum-Angel-Healing® applies fundamental concepts of quantum physics to perform healing. It works hands-on or at a distance. It uses diagnostic intuition, clairvoyance, telepathy, energy healing, and prayer. It goes beyond physical death, and integrates non-physical helpers in the process. This modality was created with angelic guidance and incorporated into a practical and teachable Certification Program. We will guide you on your path to become a *Quantum Angel Healing (QAH) Practitioner*.

We will teach you how to build a successful healing practice, which can bring you joy, happiness, fulfilment, good health, and abundance.

PLEASE VISIT OUR WEB SITES FOR

Info
Videos
Workshops
Angel-Crystals
QAH Practitioners
Meditation downloads

www.quantumangel.com
www.quantumangelblog.com